Praise for
The Serenity Solution

"*The Serenity Solution* weaves together mindfulness skills, quantum physics, and psychology in an original, fresh way to help readers bring greater awareness to their lives and create positive change. Filled with easy-to-follow exercises … it's both practical and far-reaching."

—Zoé Newman, author of *Lucid Waking*

"In his book … Keith Park offers simple, creative, yet practical strategies for solving any personal problem. Through various easy-to-learn techniques and exercises, this handy guidebook will show you how to step out of fixed and limited ways of seeing life situations and awaken to new possibilities."

—Stephen Martin, author of *The Science of Life After Death*

"This book provides readers with an excellent and gentle entryway into a life of greater inner awareness. Keith Park provides concepts, examples, and exercises that can help anyone, no matter their level of experience in meditation, to meet and solve life's problems with more mastery.

—Amy L. Lansky, PhD, author of
Active Consciousness: Awakening the Power Within

"*The Serenity Solution* is very well written and easily understood. This great little book teaches how to have a calm mind for observing, evaluating, and solving problems one encounters in daily living."

—Neil W. Crenshaw, PhD, author of *You Can Develop Pure Awareness*

"Keith Park's book *The Serenity Solution* is a wonderful book to read. Inspiring and practical, anyone seeking to solve a problem can quickly begin doing the exercises and benefit greatly from them."

—Elizabeth McAdams, PhD, President of the
International Foundation for Survival Research

"*The Serenity Solution* provides the educated reader a concise method of contemplative thinking for use in resolving emotional issues. Dr. Park describes in logical terms the controlled thought process[es], including meditation, that can provide clarity, produce desired results, and achieve goals."

—Natalie Reid, PhD, author of *5 Steps to a Quantum Life*

"Keith Park writes lucidly and powerfully about the ways to attain and use 'calm focus' to live a successful and meaningful life."

—Lynn A. Robinson, author of *Divine Intuition*

THE
SERENITY
SOLUTION

About the Author

Keith Park, PhD, is a licensed psychologist and a nationally-certified coun-selor currently practicing in Southern California. He holds a master's degree in perception and a doctorate in psychology with an emphasis in hypnosis and consciousness.

In addition, Dr. Park is the founder and director of Solutions Counsel-ing (a solution-focused-based counseling service) and Inner Life Meetings (a small group forum), both of which are devoted to helping people discover and develop their own inner potential and life goals.

THE
SERENITY
SOLUTION

*How to Use
Quiet Contemplation to
Solve Life's Problems*

KEITH PARK, PHD

Llewellyn Publications
Woodbury, Minnesota

FIRST EDITION
First Printing, 2013

Book design by Bob Gaul
Cover design by Lisa Novak
Cover image © iStockphoto.com/13684317/Pawel Gaul
Editing by Nicole Nugent
Interior art © Llewellyn art department

Llewellyn Publications is a registered trademark of Llewellyn Worldwide Ltd.

Library of Congress Cataloging-in-Publication Data
Park, Keith, Ph. D.
  The serenity solution: how to use quiet contemplation to solve life problems/Keith Park, PhD.
    pages cm
  Includes bibliographical references.
  ISBN 978-0-7387-3678-5
  1. Thought and thinking. 2. Contemplation. 3. Meditation. 4. Problem solving. I. Title.
  BF1999.P295 2013
  158.1—dc23
                          2013013191

Llewellyn Publications
A Division of Llewellyn Worldwide Ltd.
2143 Wooddale Drive
Woodbury, MN 55125-2989
www.llewellyn.com

Printed in the United States of America

To Mom and Aunt Joanne, my spiritual connections;
Dad, my foundation;
and Amy, my warm and patient companion.

Contents

Acknowledgments   xvii

Introduction   1
  How This Book Came About   5

Part One: Calm Focus and Problem Perception

One: Focus Determines View of a Problem
and Its Solution   9
  Focus as Lens and Filter   11
  Autofocus   14
  Calm Focus Opens Views   16

Two: The Focusing Continuum   19
  No Focus   20
  Hyper Focus   20
  Common Signs of Fixed Focus   22
  Avoid the Extremes   25
  Calm Focus Is Optimal Balance   26

Part Two: Problem-Solving Advantages of Calm Focus

Three: Flexible Focus Control   35
  Rating Focus Control   41

Four: Broadening Awareness—The Detached
   Observer Mode   43
   *Situation Overview: Extracting the Central
      Factor   44*
   Opening Access to Background Information   46

Five: Concentrating Awareness—Up-Close
   Immersed Mode   61
   Factors that Enhance a Solution State   66
   Physiological Effects of Immersion   69

**Part Three: Solution Targeting:
A Two-Phase Problem-Solving Strategy**

Six: Overview   83
   Targeting Questions   85

Seven: Zooming Out and Framing
   Overall Bearings   87
   Troubleshooting the Target   88
   Framing the Overall Situation   95
   Example Framing Dialogue   98

Eight: Zooming In On the Target Solution   105
   Identifying Target Markers   106
   Pinpointing the Next Step   110
   Target-Resolving Dialogue   112

Nine: Landing and Staying On Target   117
   Ongoing Target Monitoring   118

Part Four: Accessing Broader Mind

Ten: Harvesting Solutions from
Broader Mind   123
The Quantum Connection   125
An Evolving, Interconnected Universe   129
Thought Reception   130
Thought Transmission   132
Enhancing Thought Reception and Transmission   137
Thought Research   143
Harvesting Broader Mind Exercises   144

Eleven: Observing from Broader Mind   151
Identifying a Fixed View   153
Zooming Out of a Fixed View   154
Mind Versus Brain   157

Twelve: Tying It All Together   165
Practice, Practice, Practice   166
Defining a Life Goal   167

Glossary   173

Research in Distant Mental Effects   181

References   183

List of Exercises

1.1: Observing Your Focus   17

2.1: Entering a Calm Focus   29

3.1: Settling Focus   37

3.2: Redirecting Focus   38

3.3: Breaking Fixed Focus   39

4.1: Opening Focus   52

4.2: Expanding Body Awareness   53

4.3: Opening Focus in Daily Life/
   Maintaining Situational Awareness   54

4.4: Thought Streaming   56

4.5: Identifying the Central Factor   57

5.1: Target Detailing   72

5.2: Imagery Immersing   73

5.3: Evoking a Solution State   74

5.4: Evoking a Healthy State   79

7.1: Framing Overall Bearings   100

8.1: Resolving the Target   114

10.1: Tuning In to the Broader Mind   144

10.2: Dialoguing with the Broader Mind   145

10.3: Utilizing Inner Insights to Produce a
   Solution State   148

11.1: Broadening Inner Space   161

11.2: Identifying and Defusing Auto Reactions   161

List of Illustrations

1.1: The Vase/Faces Illusion   13

2.1: Optimal Zone of Performance   27

4.1: The Central or Common Factor   45

4.2: Areas of Mind   48

6.1: The Solution-Targeting Process   84

9.1: Target Chart   119

To the mind that is still, the whole universe surrenders.
—Lao Tzu

Acknowledgments

The Serenity Solution is the result of several contributions that I would like to acknowledge. First, this book would not be if not for Angela Wix, my acquisitions editor at Llewellyn. Thank you, Angela, for your faith in the book, insight and guidance, and speedy and always helpful responses to my many questions.

I would also like to thank Laura Graves and Nicole Nugent, my production editors, for their expertise in the preparation of the rough and final drafts of the book's text. *The Serenity Solution* is an easy read in part because of their knowledgeable input and insightful elaborations.

The beautiful cover and interior layouts are the creative work of Lisa Novak, my cover designer, and Bob Gaul, my production designer. Also, thank you to Kat Sanborn, my publicist, for presenting *The Serenity Solution* to the world, as well as all those at Llewellyn Worldwide who took part in making this book happen.

I would also like to thank those authors who were kind enough to provide endorsements of the book, including Stephen Hawley Martin, Elizabeth McAdams, Natalie Reid, Lynn Robinson, Neil Crenshaw, Zoé Newman, and Amy Lansky.

Finally, I would like to thank Milton Erickson and the Solution Focused Therapy community for inspiring me as a counselor. Much of the ideas presented in the Solution Targeting section of this book are in keeping with their strategic, goal-oriented, and strength-based approach to counseling.

In addition, I would like to thank the brilliant physicist David Bohm for his theories on a deeper, implicate order and the holographic nature of the universe. His ideas were ahead of their time.

To all of you, I am very grateful.

Introduction

*Few things are brought to a successful issue by impetuous
desire, but most by calm and prudent forethought.*
—Thucydides, Greek historian

In this book, I will share with you a variety of ideas and exercises that will help
you harness a calm focus and consciously use it as a tool to solve problems and
create the life you want. With a proficient use of calm focus, you can do away
with the fixed negative views that maintain fear and sadness and bad behaviors
and instead bring about joy and peace and better health and relationships.

Though there are many books on the topic of problem solving—and
even on focus control or meditation—very few instruct you how to use your
focus in specific ways to solve problems. *The Serenity Solution* both teaches you
how to condition an observant focus and how to use this focus flexibly to solve
life's problems, including work, finance, health, and relationship issues.

This book's major emphasis is on how to maintain a calm, observant state
of mind so that you may be more aware of your focus when approaching life
situations. You will thus be better able to see more options in getting past difficulties and reaching desired outcomes.

Some of the ideas and strategies you will learn here are not new; they have been used for thousands of years by great thinkers and problem solvers the world over. Yet they are distilled here as a simple and ready-to-use guide. As you read, you will discover helpful hints, age-old wisdoms, and exercises that can be applied to any problem. The exercises will also help you increase the range of your thinking and improve your problem-solving ability.

Some of the things you will learn are how to

- slow down and be more observant of life situations and your reactions to them;

- increase control of your thoughts and feelings;

- size up situations before acting; and

- open yourself to insight into problem situations.

In addition, you'll hear examples from clients in my private practice (whose names have been changed to protect their privacy) that may help clarify and inspire your use of calm focus.

Moreover, you'll learn how to use calm focus to tune into your broader inner mind and harness its informative and transformative power. When a calm focus is turned inward, it can unleash much more potential than we can otherwise. We will explore how and to what degree we can harness this power.

As you read this book, put aside your preconceived notions of how you believe your mind should work and simply consider some of the concepts and exercises presented. I assure you, the exercises are easy, safe, and fun to do! Perform these exercises on a daily basis and watch your skill in calm focus grow stronger, along with its benefits. Like any skill, calm focus takes practice, and this requires quieting your thoughts and monitoring yourself and your situations on a regular basis.

The Serenity Solution is divided into four parts. Part One explains how focus works to create our perceptions of problems and outlines the importance of calm focus in solving problems. In particular, we will look at the connection between arousal level and our perception of problems, and at calm focus as the optimal state for the flexible awareness of problems and their solutions.

In Part Two, we will explore the three major problem-solving advantages of calm focus. The first is flexible focus control, which creates the condition for the next two advantages: broadening awareness and concentrating awareness. Broadening awareness enables us to gather information about problems and observe them objectively, while concentrating awareness enables us to immerse ourselves in important details needed to solve a problem. Together, these three problem-solving advantages increase our chances of reaching viable solutions.

Part Three introduces a problem-solving technique called Solution Targeting, which employs the ideas and techniques learned in Parts One and Two. This section is a practical guidebook on how to apply calm focus (and its two major advantages of broadening and concentrating awareness) in real-life situations.

And finally, in Part Four, we look at the deeper, broader mind and its connection to a larger capacity for solutions (and quite possibly the universe itself!) as well as the means by which we might harness this larger awareness for solutions.

Though *The Serenity Solution* is divided into four parts, it can be classified into two major areas. The first area comprises Parts One through Three, which cover the basics of calm focusing and lay the foundation for the more advanced skills in Part Four.

In particular, Parts One through Three teach basic meditative skills; this includes *mindfulness* (which we describe here as broad awareness) and intention control (which we call concentrated awareness). Mindfulness is a state of mind where we have greater awareness of our focus and thoughts, as well as access to broader insights, and this awareness then allows us to concentrate our focus on the best solutions or intentions. *Intentions* are desires for specific outcomes, and they can have significant effects on our lives when we dwell or concentrate on them. They can be conscious or subconscious. When they are subconscious and unwanted, we call them fixed notions, confirmation biases, or self-fulfilling prophecies.

In Parts One through Three, we learn how to be aware of and control our intentions so that we can consciously create the ones we want and produce solutions that get us out of problems. Here we explore how consciously controlled immersion in detail, or the act of *visualization*, leads to desired intentions. This prepares us for Part Four, where we learn how to use small but significant quantum effects to produce the most effective intentions.

As we will learn in Part Four, the universe at its fundamental level (the quantum level) exists as a field of possibility, and one of the things that can produce specific realities from this field is our intentions. It is our focused thoughts that are the active ingredients in prayer, visualization, positive thinking, faith healing, and the popular concept known as the Law of Attraction, which basically states that what we focus on with conviction we tend to draw into our lives—our dominant thoughts find a way to manifest.

Overall *The Serenity Solution* shows us how we can use the two main skills of broad mindfulness and concentrated thought or intention to overcome problems and create desired outcomes. Broad or mindful awareness opens us up to solution insights and keeps us oriented to our target objectives, and concentrated intentions create the steps we need to reach these objectives.

Throughout this book, exercises are provided that build on these basic concepts. The exercises offer you an opportunity to test and hone broadening and concentrating skills. As you learn these skills and perform the exercises presented, you may want to record your observations in a journal. This will help you keep track of your progress as well as highlight patterns in your thinking and overall responses.

....

Calm Focus and Problem Solving

Observation of successful problem solvers in action reveals that a calm focus opens access to solutions. From these observations, researchers have found that solutions arise best when problem solvers

- take time to reflect on a problem;

- ponder more deeply about a problem;

- shift their focus often to look at a problem from multiple angles; and

- trust their hunches.

In contrast, those who spent the least amount of time in calm focus came up with the least number of solutions.

....

How This Book Came About

The genesis for the ideas presented in *The Serenity Solution* began while I was working on my master's degree in perception. Perception is a field of study in psychology that explores the underlying mental processes involved in how we make sense of our world, particularly how the mind organizes stimuli into meaningful information. The two fundamental processes the mind uses to organize the perceived world are synthesis and analysis, which are related to the broadening and concentrating awareness concepts presented in this book.

I explored these two states during my doctoral work in hypnosis and noticed that the detached, observant state of mind is usually accompanied by attention to a wider range of stimuli, whereas the immersed or trance-like state is usually associated with attention to a narrower range of stimuli. The biofeedback researchers George Fritz and Les Fehmi also explored these two modes of consciousness (which they call open and narrow focus) and documented their effects on the body.

Today in my work as a counseling psychologist, I keep these two fundamental processes in mind as I work with clients. We typically work by alternating between gathering a broad view of a client's problem with concentrating on specific solutions, goals, and actions. Part Three of the book presents an overview of this back and forth, which I call Solution Targeting. Solution Targeting focuses on constructing one's destiny and identifying unique strengths to shape that destiny as well as on present actions and solutions, rather than concentrating on problems and how these problems developed in the past (which is common among older approaches to change).

Does Solution Targeting work? My clients tell me so. After eighteen years of work as a hypnotherapist, wellness counselor, and psychologist, I continue to get calls, letters, and referrals from clients attesting to how helpful it has been for them. Now you too can test these ideas and techniques out for yourself and let them work for you. Let's begin!

PART ONE

Calm Focus and Problem Perception

ONE

Focus Determines View of a Problem and Its Solution

People are disturbed not by things,
but the view they take of them.
—Epictetus, Greek philosopher

The purpose of this book is to teach you how to use a *calm focus* in order to solve problems. Problems—such as work and finance issues, health concerns, and relationship conflicts—are a normal part of life. They are typically exacerbated by our difficulty in seeing ways out of these troubles. It's a vicious cycle where a problem limits our options, and our lack of options make a problem appear worse. But a calm focus can make it easier to see those options.

We've all experienced a calm focus at one time or another. Consider for a moment an argument with a friend. At times, when we hear unkind words, we jump to the conclusion that we were insulted; we become angry. At other times, we may stand back and look at the situation from other angles: perhaps our friend misspoke or we simply misunderstood. If so, we may approach the situation in a wholly different manner.

In the first reaction, we are using a hard, narrow focus. In the second one, we are using a calm focus. Unlike a hard, narrow focus, a calm focus enables us to look at a situation from a broader view; as a result, we have more options and recourses available to us.

....

The Elephant and the Six Blind Men

There's an old story in India about six blind men who went to see the prince's newly arrived elephant. None of them knew what an elephant was and so were curious. One by one they approached the elephant. One felt the elephant's side and thought an elephant was like a wall. The next touched its trunk and thought an elephant to be like a snake. The third grabbed the tusk and thought it was like a spear. The fourth a leg and thought tree. The fifth an ear and thought fan. And the sixth touched the elephant's tail and thought it was like a rope.

Now, each was partly right and partly wrong, but they failed to understand the larger truth of the elephant. They could get this only by moving around the elephant and touching all of its parts.

If we, like the six blind men, fail to size up a situation and look at it from a broader perspective, we too will fail to see what we're really dealing with. We thus will not know how to best react. A calm focus makes it more likely that we will shift and see a problem from multiple views, thereby opening the way to a solution or solutions.

....

Calm focus is an optimal state of mind for solving problems because it offers a balance of arousal—an equilibrium between alertness and relaxation. When we are both alert and relaxed, we can focus on a problem, yet our focus isn't so fixed that we can't see other views.

Problems often persist because we get stuck in one view of them and can't see other options. A good example is when we're in a hurry and can't find our car keys. In this example, we're so focused on getting out the door that we don't have room to consider where we last left our car keys.

With the balance of arousal afforded by a calm focus, we need not stay stuck. We can explore a situation from multiple views before choosing the best view. For instance, in our earlier example, when we calmly disengaged from the view that our friend *meant* to insult us, we could explore the equally valid views that he may have used the wrong words, was having a bad day, or we misunderstood; from this broader vantage point, we could see the best course of action, which, in this case, would be to clarify the matter with the friend.

Psychologists, athletes, and artists call the state of calm focus being "in the zone" or "in the flow." It is where thinking and performance are most fluid and productive. As mentioned, the optimal zone of calm focus is where we can move easily between observing an activity or situation with a degree of detachment and immersing ourselves in it. The result is an increase in the range of our thinking and performance.

Calm focus is present any time we are performing a well-rehearsed physical feat, creating a work of art, or discovering a solution to a problem. Dancing is a perfect example. When you dance with calm focus, you can move easily between a broad awareness of your body in space and an immersion in the music; as a result, you move rhythmically.

Focus as Lens and Filter

Calm focus works much like a camera lens. If we adjust a camera lens between broad and narrow views of a scene, we will increase the scope of our awareness of that scene. We see the wider landscape as well as the small details. Likewise, if we calmly adjust our focus between broad and narrow conceptions of a problem, we will increase the scope of our awareness of that problem.

As you can see, the reason our focus is so important to solving problems is it determines *what* we see in a problem and *how* we will go about solving it. In particular, our focus acts as a filter for the mind, selecting and determining what gets noticed. Thus, our focus determines how we will approach a problem and what thoughts we have available to solve a problem. If our focus is limited, our awareness of the problem and its solution will likewise be limited.

....

You Get More of What you Focus On

The notion that we are what we focus on and think about is as old as man.

- The Old Testament: "As a man thinketh, so is he."

- The Hindu text Bhagavad Gita: "Man is made by his belief. As he believes, so he is."

- Buddha: "The mind is everything. What we think we become."

- The Greek philosopher Plato: "We become what we contemplate."

- And the English poet John Milton in his work *Paradise Lost*: "The mind is its own place and in itself can make a heaven of hell—a hell of heaven."

....

Think of our camera lens again. Just as the scope and direction of the lens determines what we see through it, so too does the scope and direction of our focus determine what we entertain in our mind.

For example, if we jump to the conclusion that we are sad because people are mean to us, we will search for a solution in other people, overlooking the simple possibility that our sadness may stem from our own thoughts and perceptions. Therefore, *where* we place our focus will determine in large part whether or not we will figure a way out of a problem. If, in the above example, we can't get others to change and stop being mean to us, then we're stuck with sadness. We see no other solutions.

In fact, much of the struggle we experience in life situations comes from the limited way we are focusing on them. It is our current viewpoint at any moment, rather than any other factor, that gives us the illusion a problem is insurmountable.

This is evident nowhere more than in my private practice. In my role as a counselor, clients bring me all kinds of problems, yet invariably, most of these problems stem from a limited focus. When clients learn how to use their focus effectively, they often start to see these problems dissolve.

Most of us are familiar with perceptual illusions or drawings that have two meanings depending on how you view them. One of the most classic ones is the vase/faces illusion. Depending on where you place your focus, you can see either two faces looking at each other or a single vase in the center.

Illustration 1.1: The Vase/Faces Illusion

So it is with life situations. Often, like this perceptual illusion, life situations are ill-defined and can have multiple meanings depending on your perspective. Two people may suffer the same circumstance—the loss of a job or illness—yet one sees it as a challenge, whereas the other sees it as the end of his or her world.

As you can see, problem solving can become hampered when we hold on to the same view and do not change it. We end up getting more of what we focus on. Psychologists call this *confirmation bias*; that is, when we're locked into a single view, we tend to continue to see only those aspects of a situation that confirm this view. In short, we see what we want to see. For example, if our view of people is that they are unfriendly, we will tend to act defensively and cause others to act in kind, thus confirming our bias that people are unfriendly.

We will discuss how this common tendency can trigger not only overt actions that create a self-fulfilling prophecy but also subtle quantum effects when we discuss the power of thoughts and intentions in chapter 10: Harvesting Solutions from Broader Mind.

Autofocus

One common reason we stay stuck in a fixed view of a problem (and why a problem persists) is that we don't pay attention to what it is we are focusing on. We allow our focus to run on autopilot, or *autofocus*. As a result, we typically spend our days looking at our life situations in the same old way, oblivious to the fact that there are other ways to see them and escape from fixed patterns of living.

Autofocusing is frequently used because it allows us to go about our daily routines without much effort—our brains are inclined to expend as little effort as possible to get us through the day. After repeated dealings with situations in our lives, we start to favor certain views and reactions. Eventually, we stop seeing what's really there and see only what we expect to see; that's our *target biases*. The result is an easy but mindless habit of responding. In a sense, we behave much like robots with fixed programming.

Obviously, this is not a good state for problem solving because we're likely to continue to see and approach a problem the same way, overlooking alternate views that may lead to a solution. We are limited to only a few conditioned thoughts and actions.

You can be pretty sure that if someone is complaining about the same things over and over again, asking "Why does this keep happening to me?" or "Why do I keep feeling this way?" they are running on autofocus. This person is fixating on the same old aspects of a difficulty while overlooking other views and possible solutions. Left unchecked, autofocus is the biggest barrier to happiness, and it results in such unpleasant states as fear, anger, and sadness.

A client, Janine, had become quite frustrated with her at-home interactions with her husband. She noticed that every time they talked about important issues, such as finances or parenting, they would get into a fight. These fights went on for a while, and Janine began to think maybe she would be better off alone. I asked her to pay attention to when these fights occurred and exactly how they began. Gradually, she noticed a pattern. Conversations would start off good but soon devolve into fault-finding and defensiveness.

I instructed Janine to change the pattern. Instead of her usual reaction of debating who was to blame for their individual differences, she began looking for ways to fix the problem, such as asking her husband, "What can we do to make this right?" or "How can we work as a team on this matter?" By taking this new approach, her husband was soon active in helping her set family goals instead of fighting her on them.

In this case, Janine found her solution by stepping out of autofocus. We can do the same. The key is to be more observant of our usual patterns.

Calm Focus Opens Views

In order to solve a problem, we must change our view of it. As the brilliant scientist Albert Einstein once said, "No problem can be solved from the same level of consciousness that created it." To solve a problem, we need to step out and observe it fully. We do this through a calm focus.

A calm focus offers you one of the greatest advantages to solving a problem: its ability to broaden your awareness. When we broaden awareness, we in effect stand back and observe a situation without bias. We can see other options. For example, from our earlier illustration of believing that people are generally not nice, if we stand back and observe that people can be both unfriendly and friendly, we might not act defensively ourselves. We may therefore earn friendlier reactions from people, lessening the perceived problem.

We call this broadening of awareness being in a *detached observer mode.* Other names for it are conscious focus, mindfulness, meta-cognition, and situational awareness.

The ability to be in an observer mode and reflect on things is what separates us from robots and other animals. Unlike machines and animals, we humans can look at our thoughts and actions, see beyond our current programming, and change our behavior. We are not fused with our experiences; this is what has given us the ability to control our destiny and create civilization.

Every great thinker throughout history shared one thing in common: each stepped out and observed their thinking. It is the most direct path to illumination and a way out of any problem. It is also what great mystics and spiritual leaders have been referring to throughout the ages when they tell us to awaken and recognize our greater Self.

What mindful observing gives us is free will—the capacity to choose. There is an old saying we use in counseling: "Awareness is the first step to change." When we step back and open our awareness of a problem, we then have knowledge of it and can do something about it. It is no longer out of our sight and control.

We will explore further how we disengage from our thoughts and stay in this observer mode in later chapters. For now, try the exercise below to get started.

Exercise 1.1: Observing Your Focus

The best way to begin solving problems is to observe where you are placing your focus. We all have the ability to step aside and watch the content of our thoughts. In the following exercise, you will find that observing your thoughts can be enlightening.

1. Close your eyes for a moment and notice what's going on inside. The first thing you may notice is that your mind is continually going. Thinking is a nonstop activity. These are the details of your life.

2. Next, close your eyes for another few moments and pay attention to the *mode* of your thinking. For example, notice if you are talking to yourself or picturing things in your head. Then open your eyes and notice if you were aware of using either or both modes. Did you use one mode more than the other or both about the same? Did you hear in your mind or watch?

3. Finally, close your eyes for a minute and observe where you're placing your focus; this is the direction of your thinking. As you observe, you may notice that your focus shifts frequently from one target to the next. At one moment, you might be focusing on the present and what you have been reading; at another moment, your focus may stray to an experience in the past or to a future anticipation, or your focus may travel to a particular target, such as a person, event, emotion, or body sensation.

What direction did your focus go? Did you stay predominantly in the present or did your focus go elsewhere? Was there a particular thought or target you kept returning to?

You might want to record your findings in your journal. A journal will help you see where you are now as you begin to learn to observe and control your focus as well as how you are doing as you move along with the other exercises in this book.

TWO

The Focusing Continuum

The language of excitement is at best picturesque merely.
You must be calm before you can utter oracles.
—Henry David Thoreau

Our ability to focus calmly and flexibly and increase our solution-finding ability is tied to our arousal levels. *Arousal* here refers to our degree of alertness. In order to focus flexibly, we must not have too little or too much arousal. If we were to scale arousal from low to high, we would see that we have a continuum from no focus to hyper focus, but neither extreme is beneficial; it's that "sweet spot" in the middle we must strive for.

No Focus

At the low end of awareness or arousal we have drowsiness and a dissolving of focus. In this simple state, our thoughts wander randomly and are not controlled or directed. We are passive, not committed to any one thing, and we accept whatever comes into our mind. We daydream.

In terms of problem solving, this is not a good state to be in. Some level of control is needed to recognize a problem and sustain thought about it long enough to solve the problem.

Hyper Focus

At the other end of the arousal spectrum from no focus we have a state of high arousal and hyper focus, as is usually experienced under strong emotion—excitement, fear, anger, or frustration. Hyper focus results in three fruitless states: premature focus, fixed focus, and scattered focus.

In this hyper state, we quickly lock onto a perceived threat and exclude everything else from our awareness; this is the deer-in-the-headlights reaction, or a hard single-point focus. We call this act of narrowing in on a single view *premature focus*. Premature focus happens often when we deal with a persistent problem. In this case, we tend to focus on the most obvious or familiar parts of the problem; that is, we jump to the same conclusions. It is when someone says, "Oh, I know what this is about; this is about you lying to me again," or any variation thereof.

Premature focus is a major obstacle to problem solving because it not only limits our view of a problem, but it happens quickly. Most of us aren't even aware that we've done it. The speed and intensity with which we zoom in depends on the strength of the emotion we feel. The result is that we can quickly become cut off from other views, left with an impoverished view of a problem without even really knowing it.

Edward de Bono, in his book *Lateral Thinking*, calls premature focus "vertical thinking." According to de Bono, a vertical thinker is one who seeks a solution from the first view he sees. Typically, the first view is a familiar, habitual one. In contrast, one who looks at a problem from different angles before attempting to solve is one who is using "lateral thinking." As a result, lateral thinking tends to produce insights and unusual solutions that are unavailable to vertical thinkers.

For example, what word do you associate with the following set of words: *foot, hand,* and *eye?* If you responded by saying *body,* you are using vertical thinking to arrive at the most common association for these words. If, however, you said *ball*—as in football, handball, or eyeball, which are less common associations—you are likely using lateral thinking. Life is sometimes like this, asking us to go "outside the box" for an answer other than the typical one. It usually takes a little consideration of alternate views before we can land on a lateral or nonobvious answer.

In addition to (and because of) premature focus, hyper focus also tends to lead to two other types of unproductive focus: fixed and scattered. A *fixed focus* occurs when we hold onto a view of a problem and do not let go of it; this results from the strength of our arousal and a premature focus eliminating any competing views that might help us think about the problem in other ways. Lacking competing views, our single view (illusion) starts to seem like the absolute truth, and so we are less likely to challenge it. We therefore get more of the same. It's like seeing only the faces and not the vase in our earlier example. Once you've locked onto the image of the faces, it is difficult to unfix your focus to see the vase. A hard, fixed focus is also typically employed to distract from or ward off distressful thoughts and situations. Our brains use it to immerse us in a diversionary activity so that we can avoid the problem at hand. (See the next section: Common Signs of Fixed Focus.)

Likewise, a *scattered focus* results when we engage in premature focus repeatedly. Under strong emotion and a state of heightened arousal, we scan the environment and repeatedly target potential threats, rewards, or ways to avoid threats. We feel hypervigilant, attending to all stimuli shallowly. As a result, we become easily diverted, prone to mental conflict and indecisiveness. We have a busy, racing mind, or what psychologists call *cognitive overload.*

The end result of an overuse of hyper focus is a great deal of stress and chaos and a lack of oversight of our lives. We lose the ability to stand back and look at the totality of our thoughts and actions and where our lives our heading as a whole. It's like being lost in the trees, unable to see the forest. We can't see what's most important.

Common Signs of Fixed Focus

Lack of focus is generally easy to sense in yourself, as is scattered focus—you either think about nothing or can't stop thinking about everything. Fixed focus, however, can be insidious. There are several clear signs we are fixed in our view of a situation.

Negative Emotion

The most obvious sign that someone is fixed in their view of a situation is when they experience a persisting emotion like fear, anger, frustration, sadness, guilt, or resentment. These emotions are specific signs that the person is fixating on the faults of others or themselves and/or their circumstances while excluding other possibilities.

If you are experiencing any one of these emotions on a persistent basis or are saying things like "What if the worst happens?" or "Why bother when things always turn out the same?" or "Why does this always keep happening?" you can be sure you're in fixed focus. You keep seeing the same tired obstacles, robbing yourself of new options for change.

Doubt, Confusion, and Indecision

Overwhelming confusion, doubt, and indecision are signs that we are too close to a problem. We're lost in its details. As result, we can't see a clear way out. Again, it's like we're lost in the trees, unable to see the forest.

Common reasons for this type of confusion, doubt, and indecision are a lack of experience in simplifying problems, an inability to weed out the unnecessary, and a tendency to disregard one's own inner wisdom.

Body Aches and Pains

Another sign that our focus is fixated on a single view is body tension manifested as aches and pains. Too often we focus on external demands and ignore the warning signs brewing in our bodies in response to these demands. Left unchecked, this tension can knock off the body's natural balance and disorganize it.

On the other hand, a focus away from external demands and onto the body can begin to redirect balance.

Avoiding and Sabotaging

Avoiding and self-sabotaging are also common, ineffective approaches to problem solving that result from a fixed view. We think that an obstacle is too difficult to surmount, so it's best not to try anyway. As a result, we engage in diversionary activities—busywork, watching TV, lounging around, shopping, overeating, drinking, and other addictive behaviors—in order to avoid our problems. The diversionary activity's main purpose is to help us take our mind off the uncomfortable thoughts and feelings associated with our difficulty (e.g., "Oh, this is gloomy. I need to talk about something else. That reminds me, I need to do my laundry."). This may help in the short term, but eventually the diversion becomes just another obstacle to finding a solution to the original problem.

We may also actually sabotage our attempts at resolution. On a basic level, we're fixed on the idea that we cannot overcome this problem; we're so fixated on failure that we subconsciously find ways to bring about that failure. It's the Law of Attraction or a self-fulfilling prophecy.

Labeling

Labeling is another form of fixed view that refers to the act of applying static labels or titles to our difficulties (e.g., "I have a worry problem," or "I'm just a loner"). As we will see later, labels sometimes can help us get a conscious handle on our inner experiences ("Am I feeling fear or anger right now?"), but too often we use labels to define our problems, which can pose an obstacle to change because it creates a perception that the problem is permanent.

We will have a better chance of finding solutions to our problems if we define the problems as ongoing processes of thinking and acting rather than as static states (e.g., "I am presently worrying myself with my thinking" rather than "I'm a worrywart"). By focusing on the process of what we can think and do differently to change our situations, we put things under our control. This control is preferable to simply labeling and explaining away our situations.

Complaining, Blaming, Insisting, and Wishing

Complaining, blaming, insisting, and wishing are unproductive behaviors that indicate a fixed view. These things all involve the repeated act of expressing our displeasure about a situation while doing nothing to change it. We tend to engage in these behaviors when we feel incapable of solving a problem and so resign ourselves to at least getting things off our chest. Since these behaviors bring some temporary relief, we may engage in them repeatedly. But, unfortunately, complaining does not solve the problem and is only another distraction from finding potential solutions.

Complaining, blaming, insisting, and wishing leave us waiting passively for people and circumstances to change. If, for example, a man complains that he's painfully shy and that annoying people won't simply leave him alone, he's going to be waiting a long time for all of society to fall in line with his complaint. How should everyone else know what this one person is unhappy about? And why should others act if he won't?

We can instead empower change by taking action ourselves; our thoughts and actions are the only things we have direct control over. We'll have a better chance at change if we think and act our way toward it rather than simply waiting, complaining about it, or wishing for it: waiting to attend parties until he feels less fearful, blaming his isolation on a lack of suitable acquaintances, complaining that he has few friends, or wishing he were a more sociable person. The man would be better served by seeking help for his social difficulties or trying to change his label of himself as a shy person.

By figuring out what *we* can do to make things better despite our circumstances, we take charge of the situation and increase our chances of getting what we seek. We can monitor ourselves and the situation, and if we find ourselves complaining or insisting that people or things be a certain way, we can shift our focus to an empowered position by asking ourselves this question: "Instead of waiting for change, what can I do to change things?"

The areas in our life we complain about the most or feel most stuck or trapped in are the areas we are likely viewing in a fixed way. These are the areas we need to closely monitor in order to change our thoughts and actions.

Be on the lookout for judging or criticizing thoughts (e.g., "Why must things always be this way?" or "Why does he always create such a fuss?"); complaining about the past instead of owning our power to change the present ("I can't get over what happened"); or demanding that things be a certain way instead of trying to change them ("I shouldn't have to take care of this").

Avoid the Extremes

As you can see, problem-solving performance decreases at the low and high ends of the arousal continuum—at both no focus and hyper focus. Although hyper focus is used much more in our busy modern lives than no focus, neither of them is useful for problem solving. Both no focus and hyper focus prolong suffering because we either don't have any view of a problem (no focus, passivity) or we can't let go of an unhelpful view of a problem (hyper focus, fixity).

Moreover, both extremes put us in autofocus. In each state, we lose our sense of self—that observer part of us that typically monitors our ongoing experience. We become fused or immersed in our experience.

In low arousal, when we have little or no focus, we lose ourselves in wandering thought. In this case, we have lost sense of time, self, and our surroundings. Daydreaming is obviously bad for problem solving in that we may not realize that we even have a problem, much less any plans of action on how we will solve a problem.

In high arousal, when we experience hyper focus, we are so captured by the object of our focus that we can't think of anything else; this happens frequently when we are having a difficult time and lash out at someone for little or no reason. Here, in this case, we get so caught up in our defense against the difficult time that we lose sight of our reaction and behavior. We feel assaulted and so saw an assault where there was none.

Therefore, when in autopilot either at low or high arousal, we either are not reacting or are blindly reacting to the situation before us.

Calm Focus Is Optimal Balance

Where we seek to operate when solving problems is in the middle zone of the focusing continuum. Here, we have moderate levels of arousal, or the relaxed alertness we call calm focus. Calm focus is the optimal balance of focus control. With it, we can loosen excessive tension and control of our focus, without letting go of all control, in order to focus flexibly to a problem and see multiple views of it.

As shown in this diagram, when we work in the optimal zone of calm focus, we can control our focus and shift it along a broad–narrow dimension:

LOW AROUSAL	OPTIMAL ZONE		HIGH AROUSAL
◄- - - - - -	- -►		
	Flexible Shifting <--- Broadening Narrowing--->		
no focus, too broad	calm focus, balanced view		hyper focus, too narrow
diffuse awareness	central focus with peripheral awareness		single-point awareness
passive, wandering	open, receptive	narrow, selective	rigid, fixed
	observer mode	immersed mode	

Illustration 2.1: Optimal Zone of Performance

Broadening Awareness

When we relax focus, we *de*focus, and our focus widens like a lens opening to a scene. At this point, we are in an open, receptive state of mind and can easily observe our thoughts, our bodies, and our surroundings.

To broaden our focus effectively, we must turn off the chatter and details of the mind as much as possible and pay more attention to broader information. When we do, we gain perspective on a situation and have greater access to its larger aspects. Because it gives us the overall perspective on a situation, we call this type of focus the *detached observer mode*.

Narrowing Awareness

Conversely, when we tighten focus, we concentrate like a spotlight on a narrower range of information. As a result of this closer inspection, we can examine a part of a situation in greater detail.

Doing this type of focus requires selection and effort and is therefore an active, directed state of mind. Though it eliminates our ability to observe a situation from a distance, it can bring into sharper focus important details and actions we can take in a situation. Because of its focus on details, we call this type of focus the *up-close immersed mode*.

———————

Together, these two types of focus can be quite effective at solving problems. To see how, let's look at a quick overview of how we might use a calm focus to explore a problem and its solution using this broad–narrow dimension:

Step One: We approach a problem first by entering a calm focus. As we've discussed, a calm focus allows us room between an unrestrained and an overly-restrained view of a problem, so that we may sit quietly and explore the problem flexibly from multiple angles. (See Exercise 2.1: Entering a Calm Focus at the end of this chapter for more information on how to enter a calm focus.)

Step Two: From this calm state of mind, we enter next into the detached observer mode. Here, we mentally step back and look at the major areas of our life where we are having difficulty.

As we explore these areas, we don't get caught up in any one of them or our emotions about them. We simply look at their interrelationship and pick out the major problem. We may ask ourselves, "As I look at these concerns, where does most of the problem lie? Which factor has the most influence?"

Step Three: From this oversight, we then enter into the up-close immersed mode. Here, we concentrate on the major problem area and figure out a detailed action plan to get free of it. In looking at this problem area, we may ask, "What is needed most here?" Then we begin to figure out how we might meet this need.

Don't worry. We will discuss this broadening-narrowing process and how to do each step in the remainder of this book. By the time you're done reading and trying out the exercises at the end of each chapter, you'll know exactly how to size up any problem and tackle it.

For now, think again of this broad–narrow focusing as a camera lens zooming out and in on a scene. When we zoom out, we detach ourselves from our concerns and look at them as a whole. When we zoom in, we use the context derived from the overall layout to locate and examine an important area for further study.

As another example, let's say that you are feeling sad and don't know exactly why. You may enter calm focus and explore the areas of your life where you feel unresolved; this is the detached observer mode where we see the overall context. These unresolved areas may include gaining weight, lack of interest or no desire to go anywhere, and no one to talk to. From this overall exploration, you may conclude that what's really the issue is that you are feeling lonely. If so, you would then concentrate on the solution to this issue (getting out and meeting new friends) and how you might specifically do this; this is the up-close immersed mode where we act on salient detail.

Exercise 2.1: Entering a Calm Focus

In this exercise, we are going to learn how to enter a calm focus.

1. First, find a quiet, secluded place where you can be undisturbed for ten to twenty minutes. We are able to focus most easily when there is little distraction, so shut the door, turn off the phone, dim the lights, and arrange the room so it can be a peaceful place to focus on a regular basis.

2. Next, remove any glasses or contact lenses you wear and loosen any restrictive clothing. Find a comfortable position either sitting or lying down where you can remain for the

duration of the session. Make sure you are not too tired or you might fall asleep! Remember, a calm focus is an optimal state of mind that is reached by being neither too relaxed nor too alert.

3. When you are situated, close your eyes, take three deep breaths, and relax. Once relaxed and comfortable, clear your mind and focus on what is going on inside you. Let the outside world fade into the background. You will notice that when you first close your eyes and try to relax, the exact opposite tends to happen. Our minds and bodies tend to get restless instead of quiet, and our focus may wander from thought to thought. Accept this as a normal process and do not become discouraged.

4. Focus on your breathing; this will help to keep your focus still. Start by inhaling through your nose as you relax your stomach muscles. Next, slowly exhale through your mouth as you draw in your stomach muscles. Imagine that all tension is being released through this exhale. Repeat this several times, allowing your exhale to become slightly longer than your inhale.

5. Now simply observe your breathing without altering or controlling it. Follow it like waves rolling on the shore or a pendulum swinging to and fro. Observe it going in and out. As you inhale, note the sensation of air passing through your nose. Note the sensation of air passing through your lips as you exhale. Pay attention to the difference in sensation between the two. For instance, notice how your inhale feels slightly cooler than your exhale.

6. As you follow your breathing for a while, you should begin to notice a calm descend upon you. Take note of this calm and describe it to yourself. Where in your body do you feel it?

7. When you are ready, you may open your eyes and reorient yourself to the room. Note the physical details of the room and of your senses. Take time to make a mental note of what you observed in this session. You may want to write down your observations in your journal so that you can continue to track your progress.

PART TWO

Problem-Solving
Advantages of
Calm Focus

THREE

Flexible Focus Control

To enjoy good health, to bring true happiness to one's family,
to bring peace to all, one must first discipline and control
one's own mind. If a man can control his mind he can find
the way to Enlightenment, and all wisdom and virtue will
naturally come to him.
—Buddha

The first problem-solving advantage of calm focus—and the precursor to the other two advantages—is flexible focus control. Flexible focus control is critical for solving problems because without it, we can neither hold our focus on a problem nor shift it to see multiple views of it.

Return to our camera lens analogy again. What happens when we shake a camera around? Or hold it in the same position every time we take a picture?

We get limited information. So it is with a problem when we look at it with an improper focus.

For example, worry is the result of an unsteady focus, and sadness is the result of a fixed focus. With worry, the mind starts with a known observation (e.g., a facial gesture) and leap-frogs to more and more extreme extrapolations ("I know he/she hates me. This is the end to the relationship? How can I go on?"). Whereas with sadness, the mind selectively focuses on the negative and does not entertain other views ("Why bother? It always turns out bad.")

With the flexible control provided by a calm focus, we can hold our focus steady at one point and shift it to another, thereby avoiding the extremes of leap-frogging and fixed thinking while also increasing our range of information we know about a problem ("Though I might believe at the moment that things will turn out badly, let me at least explore some avenues I might take").

Let's try a simple exercise to begin controlling our focus flexibly. Go back to the vase/faces illusion. See if you can see the vase right now and hold that view for a moment. Keep that view in your focal awareness. Now, shift your focus and see the faces. Stay calm as you shift. Then hold it there for a moment. Now shift your focus again and see the vase once more. Hold it. Now try to see the picture for what it is: as two curvy lines. Don't form it into either a vase or two faces. Remember to stay calm. Now go to the vase... then the faces... and finally back to the lines again. See how easily you can shift from one view to the other.

With practice, this handy little exercise will teach you how to "flex" your focusing "muscle." The key is to practice shifting fluidly from one view to the other and holding each view for a moment. If you can do this, you're well on your way to learning how to expand your view of a problem and its solution.

As we said earlier, a problem often involves multiple views. For example, a husband and wife may have two different views on how to discipline their children. By being able to shift and see other views, it's easier to find a unified approach to a problem. The two parents, for instance, may begin to see some benefits in each other's disciplinary approach and incorporate the best of both into one parenting method.

In the following chapters, we will practice shifting focus and seeing multiple views. To get started, try the focus control exercises in this chapter and see how well you can begin to flex your focus.

———————

In the following pages are exercises that will begin teaching you how to control your focus so that you may better utilize it to explore a problem. As we have discussed, in order to solve a problem, we must have the right view of it, and this requires focus control. The right focus will enable us to sustain thought on a problem long enough to explore it and discover a solution.

Observe the content of your mind right now as you read this sentence. Is your attention focused fully on what you're reading? Or is your mind wandering to other things? More often our focus is divided so we do not fully process or comprehend any one thing. Fortunately, we can practice controlling our focus and the direction of our thoughts. In the following two exercises, you will learn first how to rein in unproductive thought and redirect it; in the third exercise, you will learn how to break free of entrenched thought.

Exercise 3.1: Settling Focus

1. Go to a quiet, comfortable place free from distraction.

2. Sit in a comfortable, upright position and place your hands on your thighs.

3. Take three deep breaths and relax.

4. Quiet your thoughts.

5. Select a target to focus on, such as a candle flame, photograph, or piece of fruit. Put the object in front of you. This will be

your focal point. Focus on this target and nothing else. If your mind should wander, simply bring it back to your target. Think of this process as re-centering a camera frame that has strayed from its mark. Repeat this simple refocusing or re-centering as many times as needed until you can remain focused on the target for two minutes. Build eventually to five minutes.

Exercise 3.2: Redirecting Focus

1. Close your eyes and imagine an upcoming encounter that might cause you some tension. Choose something mild, like paying a bill. Let your thoughts come freely as you envision this encounter. Notice any tension rising in your body.

2. Snap your fingers and order it to stop. Imagine a big red stop sign in front of you. Cancel all inner pictures and talk. Sustain a quiet mind without any thoughts for a moment.

3. Redirect your focus to your present body sensations. Take a deep breath … release … and relax your muscles.

4. Now turn the outcome around. Replay the scenario, but this time see yourself handling the situation with calm and confidence (paying the bill on time or doing what is necessary to extend or mend it) and tell yourself, "I've got this. It's no problem."

By practicing these two simple exercises on a regular basis, you will begin to control your focus and stop unproductive trains of thought before they get going.

My client Sally uses the redirecting focus exercise to quell disagreements with her husband. Whenever she finds that she is about to react blindly and internalize hurtful statements, she imagines a big red stop sign and tells herself, "Stop. Don't internalize or own it. Instead, think: 'What is the best way to handle this situation?'" By doing so, she is staying out of autopilot (and arguments) and is getting into the habit of increasing her inner and outer peace.

Exercise 3.3: Breaking Fixed Focus

In this exercise, we're going to practice disengaging from a fixed view and seeing other views. The most common fixed views are long-held notions about the self. The goal of this exercise is to learn to step back from negative notions and entertain other viewpoints.

1. First, choose a negative belief about yourself, such as "I lack confidence" or "I am unlikable," and write it in the space provided on the next page.

2. Put this notion aside for a moment; in a relaxed state of mind, write down as many examples as you can think of that disprove this notion in the next space provided. Don't censor your thoughts at this time. Just write down any reasons you may have. Include prior examples or exceptions. For example, if you believe you lack confidence, list as many examples as you can think of from your past where you displayed some confidence, even if it was just a little bit.

3. If you can't find any examples, it's probably because you're holding tight to your negative self-image. If this is the case, write any example that comes *close* to being an exception. For example, if the negative self-image is a lack of confidence, write any examples that looked like confidence, such as a little less fear or doubt when taking action—this may include times when you spoke up, made a decision, or stuck to a decision.

4. Afterward, review your counterexamples and ask yourself, "Do I fully believe this original notion about myself? Or is it possible that I just think this from time to time?" Hopefully, if you've found enough counterexamples, your view has shifted from its original position. If not, you may still be holding firm and need to go back and find some more examples until you can move your position at least a little.

Negative Self-Notion:

Counterexamples and Exceptions:

Many clients report that of all the exercises in this book, this is the hardest one to perform. This is understandable given that most self-notions have remained unchallenged for so long that they become a fixed feature in the background of our minds, thereby conveying an aura of absolute truth. The remedy is to get into the habit of challenging these notions early and often, before they become fixed.

Rating Focus Control

Rate your ability to control your focus in the preceding exercises on a 1–10 scale, where 1 represents no ability to control and 10 stands for complete focus control. What number did you give yourself? What could you do next to raise your control up even a single point?

It is okay if you didn't do as well as you hoped on these exercises! It's a start. Just remember to practice them, as they will form the foundation for your ability to use your focus to solve problems. Practice until you can comfortably focus on your target for five minutes, break from a target when desired, and/or can rate your focus-control ability at level 8 or higher.

As with any skill, your proficiency at controlling your focus will increase with practice. In time, you should notice your ability to hold and shift focus increase. The more your focus control increases, the more you'll find success in problem solving and daily life.

FOUR

Broadening Awareness—The Detached Observer Mode

You can't see the forest for the trees.
—Proverb

The next problem-solving advantage of calm focus is broadening awareness, or reaching the detached observer mode. Once we enter into a calm focus and learn to shift it flexibly, we may begin to broaden it.

Broadening awareness has two sub-advantages. One is the ability to mentally step back and observe things in perspective; this includes looking at the larger aspects of our lives and their interrelationships. The other advantage is the ability to be receptive to inner background information. We call the first sub-advantage—seeing in perspective—*situation overview.*

Situation Overview: Extracting the Central Factor

Situation overview involves looking at the major sources of a problem and how they interact before we do anything else, so that we're sure we are focused on the real problem—the major influence in our lives—and not a tangential issue. Recall that only once we become aware of something, such as the real cause of a problem, can we then do something about it. We then have more choice and control over it.

For instance, in our earlier example of feeling sad, when we step back and look at our weight gain, lack of interest, and social isolation, we see that we are lonely. With awareness of the root problem, we are in a better position to do something about this loneliness.

Situation overview is similar to zooming out of a scene and capturing the scene's overall context. By seeing the broader relationships in a scene, we can better determine what we're dealing with and how to deal with it. When we observe our lives in perspective, we do not get caught up in any particular aspect, its details, or our emotional reactions to the scene. We simply stand back, observe, and gather information about the overall interrelationships of major factors. Recall that broad focus is an open, receptive state of mind; this is the reason we call it the *detached observer mode.*

It's wise to stand back and look at problems in perspective because too often life problems are ill-defined and involve a number of factors. There are typically external factors from multiple sources, such as work, finances, health, and relationships; and then there are internal factors, such as our perceptions and our emotional-physical reactions to these external pressures. A man may, for instance, have a problem at work and also suffer from worry, negative self-talk, and low productivity in response to his work problem.

However, not all factors in an ill-defined problem are equal in importance. Some factors contribute more to creating a problem than others, and some are a distraction to problem solving if we focus on them. For example, if a man engages in disagreement with his spouse when he's really mad at his boss, it's a distraction from the real issue, which is the working relationship with the boss.

In fact, most problems persist because we're too close to them and are focusing on the wrong factors. We can't see what the real issue is—what's causing most of the problem. Although there may be a number of contributing factors, there is often one factor that causes most of the problem. We call this factor the *central factor* as opposed to *peripheral factors*. It is the dominant influence in a problem, or the most pervasive factor.

In counseling, we call the central factor the *real problem* as opposed to the *presenting problems*. In the previous example, this would be issues with the man's boss, which may stem from an even broader factor related to feelings of insecurity at work or a negative general outlook on life.

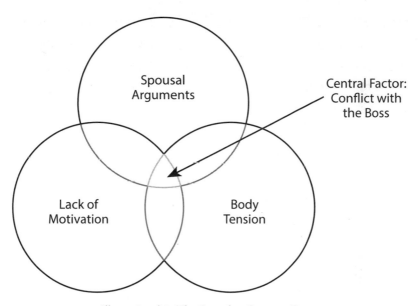

Illustration 4.1: The Central or Common Factor

The central factor typically can be found by looking at the common connection among a number of complaints. Solving a problem becomes much easier when we attend to this central factor instead of all of the other factors. It's like treating the disease instead of treating the symptoms.

In his book *Lateral Thinking*, Edward de Bono refers to the central factor as the *dominant idea* or *theme*. According to de Bono, when we are not aware of a problem's dominant idea, we can never be sure we have escaped its influence. We may take action on the problem and even think we've found a solution or way out, but in actuality we're still under the influence of this dominant idea or theme.

Identifying the central factor is also the basis for the common phrase, "A problem well-defined is one that is half-solved," coined by the American philosopher John Dewey. Again, that is to say that when we can clearly define what we're dealing with, we can better see *how* to deal with it.

Identifying the central factor ensures that we avoid being blocked by this otherwise hidden obstacle. For instance, by leaving off arguing with his spouse and acknowledging feelings of insecurity at work, the man can begin to get out from under the influence of this factor.

We will learn more about how to identify the central factor as well as look at our life situations more broadly in the exercises that follow this chapter. For now, let's look at the next sub-advantage to broadening awareness: receptivity to background information.

Opening Access to Background Information

Another common feature of broadening awareness is *defocusing*, or opening awareness to additional information. Recall that our focus works like a camera lens. A camera lens may defocus to take in a wider vista; likewise, mental defocusing may let in a larger array of thoughts from background areas of mind. Through a calm inner focus, we may observe a greater number of thoughts and thoughts that are deeper and more original.

We all have within us enough information to solve life problems—we just need to take the time to access that information. When we do, we often find the solutions we have been looking for. In fact, neuroscience provides much evidence that most of our thinking occurs outside our normal state of consciousness. Outside our focal awareness lies a larger background awareness that holds not only knowledge of our body and its processes but also knowledge of our deepest thoughts and insights. Many of the early pioneers of the mind believed this, including the Swiss psychiatrist Carl Jung. He stated in his book *Psychology and Religion* that "the unconscious mind is capable at times of assuming an intelligence and purposiveness which are superior to actual conscious insight."

We usually aren't aware of this greater information because of our typical filter that blocks out all but our immediate concerns and familiar and habitual thoughts. As a result, we tend to operate most of the time in a relatively narrow range of awareness called our *focal awareness*. We do this in order to move through our regular day-to-day life without being overloaded by information and thoughts.

However, when we relax, we may experience a defocusing and a release of background information. Thoughts may come into focal awareness as suddenly and as clearly as a flash of insight or as slowly and as subtly as a hunch or intuition. For example, we may strive in vain to recall a name only to have it pop into our heads later when showering or driving down the highway. The name was there all along—we just didn't have access to it until we relaxed. Likewise, we might suddenly get the notion that a friend is about to call right before the phone rings.

To understand the relationship between our conscious mind, or focal awareness, and larger areas of mind, consider the analogy of a spotlight illustrated on the next page. In the center of the spotlight, we see a small, bright circle; this area represents our focal awareness, which provides access to our immediate thoughts and our conscious awareness. Adjacent to

this bright inner circle are darker areas that represent access to our precon-
scious and subconscious thoughts, respectively.

Now, just as light level decreases as we move out from the bright center
of a spotlight, we also experience a decreasing ease of access to broader areas
of mind as we move from conscious thoughts to subconscious thoughts. As
we move to the outer darker areas of this illustration, we find a more extended
and diffuse awareness as well as a need for calmer, deeper focus.

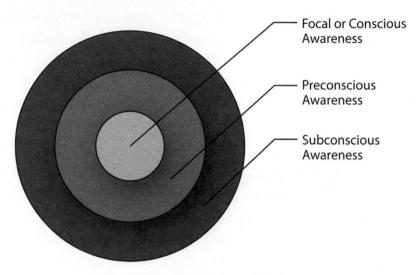

Illustration 4.2: Areas of Mind

Psychologists have studied the processes by which people gain insight or
solutions to their problems for decades now, and a common conclusion has
been reached: solutions tend to arise best when people are relaxed and not
busying themselves with the details or thinking too hard about a solution.

In fact, many of the world's greatest thinkers whose ideas have advanced
civilization over millennia—such as Plato, Aristotle, Archimedes, Galileo,
Newton, da Vinci, Mozart, Edison, and Einstein—made many of their world-
altering discoveries in a calm, relaxed state of mind.

When relaxed and not thinking about anything in particular, Thomas Edison once said his ideas came "right out of the air ... pulled out [of] space." Mozart confessed to a friend that his ideas "flow[ed] best and abundantly" when relaxed and alone without distractions, and "whence and how they come I know not." Beethoven also remarked that his ideas came unexpectedly while not doing anything in particular: "You ask me where I get my ideas, that I cannot tell you with certainty; They come unsummoned, directly, indirectly—I could seize them with my hands—out in the open air; in the woods, while walking; in the silence of the night; early in the morning." Even Einstein added, "The intellect has little to do on the road to discovery. There comes a leap in consciousness; call it intuition or what you will—the solution comes to you and you don't know how or why." The value of quiet contemplation to understanding was so valuable to the ancient Greeks that the philosopher Aristotle considered it the highest human endeavor.

Likewise, many of us have discovered solutions to our problems this way. Think about it: Did many of the solutions to your most difficult problems come when you were worrying or striving too hard for an answer? Or did they come when you finally backed off from the problem and relaxed?

Think about the time you forgot a name or misplaced an item like your car keys. Did you typically retrieve the memory when you were straining for it? Or did you retrieve it when you paused for a moment and let the memory come to you?

In fact, research into arousal and memory recall has shown a consistent link between high arousal and an *in*ability to retrieve information from memory. Presumably, relaxation leads to an opening of the usual filter that normally inhibits thoughts from background areas of the mind.

Accessing Broader Information via Open Questions

One way we can reliably access background information is through the use of *open questions*. Open questions are so named because they do not ask for a one-word or a yes/no response like *closed questions*, but instead require elaboration of a topic, and therefore get at a greater understanding of it. Open questions typically begin with the words *what, where, when,* or *how.* Example: "What's causing most of the problem? What can I do here to improve things? Where can I take action? How can I do it?" These are the same questions that reporters and detectives ask to really round out an investigation. They are the questions that give one the clearest picture of an entire situation or problem.

In contrast, we generally avoid closed questions for the reason mentioned above. Closed questions typically start with words like *can, should, did,* or *is.* Example: "Is there a reason this is happening? Can I overcome this problem?"

Compare the open question "What factor is causing most of the problem?" with the closed question "Is there a reason this happening?" As you can see, the open question asks for more information. Likewise, compare the difference between "What can I do to improve things?" to "Can I improve things?" In this case, the open question points to actions not asked by the closed question.

Therefore, what is needed to get at a solution is the right question. Our output will only be as good as our input—garbage in, garbage out, as computer programmers say. The questions we ask will determine what direction we look to for a solution and the level of output we get from our broader inner mind.

For this reason, we should avoid questions that start with the word *why,* as in "Why is this happening?" or "Why do they make me feel this way?" *Why* questions are unproductive because they seek explanations for things out of our control and do not address actions we can take to remedy a situation.

When in session, I often facilitate insight through the use of open questions. A client may be struggling with a problem and at some point go quiet and find him or herself on the verge of a thought. At this point, I usually invite the client to relax for a moment and ask the open questions "What is this? What is really seeking my awareness right now?" Many times this open questioning proves fruitful, and the client reveals a breakthrough on the issue.

Open questions can be used at any time to explore a problem, not just in session. To do this, we have to be willing to sit quietly in calm inner focus and ponder on a problem while we put away preconceived notions of what we think the answer *should* be and simply explore whatever comes to mind. By not censoring our thoughts, we provide an optimal environment for the free flow of ideas to come from our broader inner mind.

Many times, though, when these background thoughts enter focal awareness, they are vague or unformed. We may feel the urge to discard them as unimportant. However, it is in our best interest to consider even these vague thoughts, since they are coming from a larger area of mind. Often they prove fruitful to understanding and solving a problem.

Some of the ways background information may come to us are in the form of:

- words or phrases;

- symbols or imagery;

- body sensations or feelings; or

- as a general sense about things.

There are several ways to distinguish useful background information from focal thought. Useful information from our broader mind often

- addresses the real problem;

- leads to greater understanding;

- provides a simple solution;

- opens up options;

- is association with a deeper calm and sense of certainty; and

- is consistent over time.

If we get any one of these clues, we should pay attention. We can always test this advice in the light of day to see if it holds up to scrutiny.

———

Now that we've learned how to flexibly control our focus, we're going to learn how to broaden it. In the next four exercises, we will practice first how to be receptive to background information and then how to pick out the central factor in the mental noise that typically surrounds a life problem. This will prepare us for framing problems and targeting solutions in Part Three: Solution Targeting.

Exercise 4.1: Opening Focus

In this exercise, we're going to practice defocusing so that we are more receptive to surrounding information. The effect is like putting our minds in an open, neutral state. We are simultaneously aware of several targets or topics but are not focused on any one target. Defocusing not only prevents us from jumping to premature conclusions, it also prevents our bodies from gearing up and reacting to any one thing. As a result, our bodies can fully relax, and our minds can be at peace.

To defocus, perform the following steps:

1. Go back to your quiet place, remove any distractions, and sit or lie in a comfortable position where you can be undisturbed for about ten minutes. If you lay down, make sure you are not so tired that you may fall asleep. Recall that we want to be in a calm focus, which is a balance between being relaxed and alert, not sleepy or drowsy.

2. Close your eyes and cut off any visual distractions. Take a few deep breaths, quiet your thoughts, release tension, and relax.

3. Sit quietly and note the sounds and sensations around you, such as the sound of a ticking clock, air conditioner, or passing cars as well as the feel of the air and its temperature. At the same time, note the experiences going on inside of you, such as the feel of your body in the chair, your heartbeat and blood flow, and any passing thoughts and emotions.

4. Remain detached and simply observe. Do not focus on any one thing or focus on things one at a time (i.e., do not sequence targets). Simply spend a few moments accepting all things into your awareness without reacting to any one thing. Again, this is easier said than done because the mind will want to wander or engage.

5. Accept wandering and engaging as normal responses. If you should find yourself wandering or engaging, simply say to yourself, "I am wandering/engaging that," and return to observing all things at once. Observe openly for five minutes. Build up to ten minutes a day of defocusing.

Exercise 4.2: Expanding Body Awareness

In this exercise, we turn our focus inward to receive subtle information about the body.

1. Start by entering calm focus. Next, place your focus on the inner space of your body. Imagine your body as a container and your focus as a spotlight shining on all the inner parts of your body.

2. Observe patiently for a few minutes. Give your focus time to settle and the inner space to come in clearer. As you do this, you should start to notice thoughts, sensations, images, and impressions about your body that you overlooked while in an external focus. This is inner information entering into focal

awareness from deeper layers of intelligence within your mind and body. We can use this information as a way to align with these internal processes and begin to consciously control them.

3. Sit quietly now and simply note all the things in your body as you become aware of them. Accept even the slightest of sensations. Explore the inner scene like a camera lens panning around a room. Note what draws your attention. Let your inner intelligence guide you to the area needing most attention and describe the area to yourself. Ask your inner mind, "What is needed most here to begin healing this area?" and wait patiently for an answer.

4. Take whatever comes, and then open your eyes to return your focus to the room. Think about how to enact this advice.

Exercise 4.3: Opening Focus in Daily Life/Maintaining Situational Awareness

Even when we are not doing formal sessions of calm open focus, we can practice maintaining a calm observant state of mind in our normal lives. Consider the following daily observations:

1. Be aware of what is going on around you wherever you go. Note the sights, sounds, smells, and sensations around you. Again, when you find yourself wandering off or fixating on one thing, simply return to a broad awareness.

2. Stay openly aware as you monitor your ongoing activities, such as getting ready for work, driving, and doing daily chores. Focus not only on the task at hand but on what is going on around you. Note both the steps and details of what you're doing but also the effects of these actions on the world around you.

3. Take time during the day to observe what is going on inside you. What are you thinking, feeling, sensing? Are your thoughts helpful or hindering? Do you feel rushed, impatient, calm? Is there tension in your body? Where? How are you breathing? Can you take care of the things around you and observe without getting caught up in the hurried feelings? Simply stand back from the experiences and observe them with detachment.

4. Pay broader attention to those around you. Observe them without judgment. Listen not only to the words they say but to the way they say them. Notice their gestures. Avoid interrupting until they are finished talking. Shift your viewpoint and see things from their perspective. Imagine what it would be like to see the world through their eyes. Think how you would respond differently.

I give this last part of this exercise to my couples in counseling in order to improve communication. We take turns listening to and imagining what a disagreement looks like from the other partner's viewpoint. Often, this perceptual repositioning not only decreases senseless bickering and increases mutual cooperation, but it offers something new that each partner did not know about the other.

———

By practicing these initial broadening exercises, you should be able to stop autofocusing (automatic targeting and reacting to things) and stay in calm observant focus for longer periods, thereby heightening your observation skills and awareness of inner and outer experiences and opportunities. Next, we explore how to use a broad focus to gather insight to a problem.

Exercise 4.4: Thought Streaming

Another way to produce fluid insights is through a technique called *thought streaming*. In thought streaming, we pose a question and then remove our mental filter to allow an uncensored flow of information from our inner mind.

1. Choose a question you would like an answer to and then go into calm focus and pose the question to your inner mind.

2. Completely relax your mind and prepare to receive the answer. Maintain an expectant attitude and allow your thoughts to flow freely. Follow your thought stream wherever it may go. Don't censor it.

3. Review your thoughts. Make them tangible by writing down the thoughts that came up several times, stirred up emotion, or drew your attention the most. Try to find the right words to capture those thoughts that stood out the most. Be succinct. Boil them down to one sentence; this is your answer.

Thoughts:

Summary Sentence:

Exercise 4.5: Identifying the Central Factor

Finally, in this last broadening exercise, we're going to learn how to explore a current problem in our lives by calmly detaching and looking at the interrelationship of its factors. This will help us to determine the problem's central factor.

Recall that the central factor is the one factor (among many) that has the most influence on a situation. It typically is the common underlying cause of several surface complaints. For example, though a person may complain outwardly about how bad things are, being let down by others, and how nothing seems to work in his life, these may be peripheral symptoms of an underlying sense of helplessness.

To find the underlying central factor, we have to search a little deeper and broader for the answer. Often, it is the answer your inner mind delivers when you take time to ask yourself, "What is really bothering me?" To answer the question, you typically don't select every concern you have; instead, search your mind for the one factor that is having the most effect on how you feel at the moment.

Using our earlier work-conflict example, let's see how the man might find the central factor (dominant theme) in the initial mental noise that accompanies such life difficulties:

> *Things are really bad lately … everything is going wrong … I'm stressed all the time … I can't sleep … keep fighting with my wife … my neck is hurting from so much tension … my boss is always on my back … nothing is ever good enough no matter how hard I try … can I pay the bills? … I'm never going to retire … should I go to night school? … will I have the time? … losing my temper the other day wasn't good … I don't know what I want anymore … things are confusing … I have so many problems … my life's unraveling … I'm really depressed … what's wrong with me?*

Whew! It seems there are a number of factors this person feels are affecting his present situation: feeling stressed, trouble sleeping, spousal arguments, body tension, work conflict, and future security concerns, as well as concerns about his emotional state. These are the presenting complaints or problems.

Now, it is true that the person may be concerned by a number of these factors, but only *one* of them has the largest influence: conflict and insecurity at work. It is the one factor most contributing to the other factors. If it were not for insecurity at work, this person would most likely not be so stressed and short with his spouse, losing sleep, feeling tense, questioning himself, or worried about his future and other means of income.

Although the central factor or dominant theme does not appear explicitly in the person's frantic narrative, it can be deduced when we look at the complaints as a whole and tease out what is central from peripheral. A sentence like, "My insecurity at work is affecting my health, home life, financial outlook, and emotional state" fits perfectly as the dominant theme of this situation and is a concise definition of the problem. We can pretty much agree that this succinct statement increases awareness of the real problem, whereas the undefined dialogue reveals only confusion that adds to the person's suffering.

1. In the space below, jot down your thoughts about an area of your life that is troubling you right now. Just as you did in the thought-streaming exercise, and as illustrated with the work-conflict example, allow your thoughts to flow freely.

2. Next, look at these thoughts as a whole. See if any of these thoughts are related. Do you notice a common connection among any of them?

3. Try to identify the one underlying factor that might be influencing or explaining most or at least a majority of these thoughts. Write this factor down in the second space.

Thoughts/Complaints:

Central Factor:

How did you do? If you found this exercise a bit hard, don't worry. You'll have enough practice at it in Part Three: Solution Targeting. For now, let's take a look at the third problem-solving advantage of calm focus: concentrating awareness.

FIVE

Concentrating Awareness— Up-Close Immersed Mode

You can't see the trees for the forest.
—Proverb in reverse

After learning how to shift and broaden our focus, we move into the third problem-solving advantage of calm focus: concentrating awareness, or the up-close immersed mode.

Concentrated awareness is an active, directed state of mind wherein we closely examine an area selected from broad overview. Though concentration eliminates our ability to observe a situation from a distance, it can bring into sharper focus important actions we can take on a problem.

We typically employ concentration after we have broadened focus and captured a problem's central factor. This way, we're sure of targeting our efforts in the most relevant area. Here we examine the detailed actions or steps needed to free ourselves of this major influence and produce a solution.

We call concentration the up-close immersed mode because when we are in it, we shift from a detached observer of a problem into an active player/experiencer of a solution. This involves mentally projecting ourselves into the problem scenario and playing out the actions that will free us from the problem.

For example, let's say we find that the major influence (the central factor) in a problem is a lack of assertiveness. If so, we would then concentrate on the individual thoughts and actions that would produce assertiveness and thus rid ourselves of this central factor.

Immersion is the natural result of focusing on the details of something, especially a sequence of steps or actions. Moreover, mentally immersing yourself in (vividly imagining) a sequence of actions can actually produce physiological and neuromuscular responses; this is because the body does not discriminate much between actual performance and one vividly imagined. As a result, we can mentally practice solution behaviors and "trick" the body into thinking it has actually done these behaviors. You can imprint the solution steps onto your nervous system. This way, when you need them in the actual problem setting, these mentally-practiced actions will be more easily manifested. Athletes often use this technique for races, mentally "running" the race over and over again as a form of practice.

Consider what happens when we immerse ourselves in a good movie or book. We may laugh, cry, tense, relax. These events are not real, but because we make them real in our mind, our body reacts as if they are real, quickening our pulse or clenching our hands in fear. In fact, immersion is the basis for visualization, hypnosis, and the placebo effect.

We call eliciting mental and physical effects from immersion *evocation*. Evocation was popularized by the innovate psychiatrist Milton Erickson, MD. Erickson was best known for his indirect, or naturalistic, approach to hypnotic therapy. This form of therapy involved eliciting hypnotic effects—such as analgesia (inability to feel pain), amnesia, and age regression—by sharing detailed stories with clients and utilizing a client's own experiences with such events. Erickson believed that it was best to utilize a client's own experiences, since these were already well established in the client's mind and could simply be reawakened as a resource.

For example, if the therapeutic objective was to produce a lessening of perceived pain, Erickson would evoke analgesia by eliciting a client's memories of numbing coldness. In particular, Erickson would speak at length and in detail about common experiences a client might have had with exposure to cold temperatures; this would evoke a present state of numbness in the client. Afterward, the client would be offered suggestions on how to transfer this numbing experience to the painful body area.

Following in Erickson's footsteps, hypnotherapists began using evocation to elicit all kinds of resourceful states—calmness, confidence, happiness, body relaxation, and so on—by simply reminding clients of their own detailed experiences in the past with such states.

In fact, evocation of mental and physical effects with mental immersion has been used to successfully treat many conditions, most notably anxiety, depression, chronic pain, and stress-related disorders such as headaches, hypertension, cardiovascular disease, and even cancer. For more information on the physical effects of mental immersion, check out the section Physiological Effects of Immersion later in this chapter.

In the present context of problem solving, we call resourceful states *solution states* because they provide the state of mind and body needed to end a problem state. As we have seen, what creates a solution state is detail. Each solution state is comprised of a sequence of individual thoughts and actions that, when vividly played out, trigger the mental and physical effects that can end a problem state. For example, the state of assertiveness may arise to overcome a problem state of fear if we mentally immerse ourselves in the following actions: monitoring our tension level, taking a few deep breaths, releasing body tension, and telling ourselves we are confident.

The more detail we use in immersion, the more our mental blueprint approximates the actual condition we are striving for and the more real it feels to our bodies. To find this detail, we must discover the steps that will get us beyond the influence of the central factor. We find these steps by asking ourselves, "What is needed most to overcome this factor? What are the specific thoughts and actions that will produce this needed outcome?" A woman experiencing the problem state of anxiety may ask herself these questions and realize that what is needed most to overcome the anxiety is calmness, and thoughts of a quiet forest with birds singing and a gentle breeze will produce this solution state of calmness. The woman would then fill in this forest scene with as much detail as possible to make the immersion most effective. By immersing herself in the scene, her body will produce physical signs of calmness even in tense times.

To experience the visceral effects of detailed immersion, compare the difference between the two following narratives:

Narrative One

I could feel the cold autumn day as I walked along.

Narrative Two

As I moved briskly along the empty, winding path, short bursts of frosty air momentarily robbed me of my breath. The blast of wind both exhilarated me and chilled me to my bones. Though I knew my nose and ears were attached, I could no longer feel them. They had grown completely numb. All around me, I could see orange and brown leaves and smell the sharp scent of pine. The sky hung low, dark, and cloudy. Light snowflakes had just begun to fall. As I walked, twigs crackled beneath my feet. The thought then entered my mind: *autumn is here*. I accepted it with peaceful resignation.

———

As you can see, Narrative One is too general to produce a visceral reaction, whereas Narrative Two comes much closer to producing a reaction due to its greater descriptive detail.

To create the full effects of immersion, we must concentrate solely on the actions we want and no other thoughts; this requires effort and control. Often, though, when we first begin focusing on what we want, we start worrying about not getting it and actually end up focusing on what we *don't* want instead. For example, when we start focusing on peace, our thoughts may stray to fear and tension, and we end up inadvertently evoking the wrong state.

Obviously, we want to avoid immersion when we have a wrong or negative focus and encourage it when we have the right one. For this reason, we need to be observant of what we are focusing on and be sure we're focusing on the right state. Still, there's no need to fret! If you find your attention has strayed, simply return it back to your desired focus and keep it there. The exercises on focus control presented earlier should help in this regard. Plus, there are several exercises at the end of this chapter that will help to improve your concentration skills.

By mentally immersing in solution states, we can improve our response to pressure, more easily leave comfort zones, engage in new and difficult tasks, overcome challenging problems, reach greater levels of achievement, and even heal the body.

Moreover, as we will see in chapter 9, there is more we can do to enhance immersion and produce solution outcomes. In that chapter, we will learn how to construct intentions that produce quantum effects and increase our chances of manifesting desired outcomes.

Below are several factors to consider when constructing and immersing yourself in a solution state. Keep these factors in mind, as we will build upon them later, when we learn how to create these quantum effects.

Factors that Enhance a Solution State

There are several factors that are keys to evoking resourceful states. As we discussed throughout this book, the first one is a calm focus. We must be totally relaxed and undisturbed; the greater the relaxation, the greater the ability to focus inward. The other key factors are presented below. You should keep these in mind when constructing the mental picture of your desired states.

Focus On a Positive Outcome

First, you must focus on what you want, not on what you don't want. To do this, create pictures in your mind of what you want to see happen in a problem situation. Be careful to avoid thoughts about what you don't want to happen. See the situation in a positive way. If, for example, the problem is a lack of assertiveness, imagine acting and speaking confidently. Don't tell yourself, "I will not be fearful." This statement focuses on the notion that we do indeed lack assertiveness. Say instead, "I am confident in this situation."

Focus On a Present Outcome

Don't wish the outcome will happen in the future; imagine it as though it is occurring right at this moment. This sends the message to our inner minds and bodies that we are experiencing the outcome now, which will produce the physical effects we are striving for.

Focus On a Believable Outcome

Make sure you believe the outcome. If the conscious part of your mind doesn't buy the solution state as possible, it won't get past the mental filter to your inner mind, and you will lack the motivation to achieve the solution state. If, for instance, your goal seems distant, such as being happy after years of sadness, and you can't see it happening in the present, it might be best to divide the goal into intermediate subgoals. Then you can imagine obtaining each smaller goal one step at a time. To affirm each step along the way, say to yourself, "I am becoming happier each and every day, and this is my first step to getting there."

Focus On a Specific Outcome

Being specific is also important. Imagine the exact details of what you want. Recall that detail is vital to immersion effects simply because the body reacts to a vivid mental picture much as it does to the actual event. As long as your conscious mind believes it, your body will accept it.

Spend a few minutes bringing your imaginary senses into the scene and building up the mental picture. Start with the visual aspects of the solution scene, then add the auditory and kinesthetic. If you like, you can add the taste and olfactory senses as well. The more detail you can add, the more real the outcome will seem to your inner mind and body, and the easier it will be to carry out. For example, if you want to be assertive, imagine standing confidently and feeling strong in your body. Imagine the sound of your confident voice.

Focus On the Feeling

The most important sensory detail to focus on is the kinesthetic sense, or the *feel* of the outcome. We let our bodies know how they are to perform, not the other way around. Imagine that you are actually participating in the outcome state and let your body experience what it feels like to have obtained this goal.

By imagining the body performing the action, we stimulate neuromuscular responses that imprint on the nervous system. When the mental action is detailed enough, it is nearly like being there doing the activity, and our bodies will believe it is happening.

Don't forget to include emotion. Strong emotion easily slips past the conscious mind to the inner mind. Think about how you instantly perk up after hearing a compliment; the happy feeling permeates your brain very quickly. Therefore, if your desired outcome is to be assertive, for example, imagine the feeling of your body standing strong and tall along with the emotion of being proud that you are able to do so.

Focus Repeatedly On the Outcome

The next important factor to consider when evoking solution states is repetition. Each time we mentally practice our desired performance, neuro-pathways are strengthened. Each time, our simulated performance gets closer to actual performance. The result is an imprinted template of the desired performance that is more likely to be activated automatically when it is needed in the real setting.

We see this process happening in nonproductive ways with chronic negative thinking. As we think bad thoughts over time, we tend to reinforce these thoughts in our minds and bodies. But if we can produce ill effects from chronic negative thinking, the reverse should also be true—we should be able to produce healthy effects from chronic positive thinking, or mentally rehearsing desired outcomes.

Use a Trigger to Evoke the Outcome

To assist in evoking the desired performance state or outcome, use a trigger. A trigger is a snapshot of a particular action taken from the performance sequence. It can be something that represents the outcome itself, or it can be a symbol that represents the performance. For example, if the outcome is to be assertive, a representative image of this outcome may be the image of standing tall. By mentally associating this image with the desired performance repeatedly (mentally picturing yourself standing tall over and over again as you immerse yourself in the feeling of confidence), you turn the image into a trigger. This trigger can be used anytime you need it to elicit the desired performance of acting assertively. With practice, the outcome or solution state will be automatically activated as soon as the trigger is cued.

Test and Refine the Outcome

The final factor to consider when evoking a solution state is action. Without action, we have no feedback, so we can't really tell if our mental practice has been successful in producing the desired outcome. Therefore, we must test our actions in the actual problem situation.

To continue our example, you can only evaluate how close your actual performance matches your desired performance by attempting to act confidently in an uncomfortable setting. After testing yourself, determine what actions still need to be practiced or added in order to reach your desired state.

In summary, the key factors to constructing and evoking effective outcomes are to picture the end result, make it believable and specific, focus on the feeling and the picture repeatedly, create a trigger, and then test and refine the practiced performance.

Physiological Effects of Immersion

As we have seen, detailed immersion has a significant effect on the body due to the body's reaction to lifelike mental pictures. Because of this mind-body link, we have much more influence over our bodies than we realize. We not only can mentally practice desired performance, such as remaining calm in anxious situations, but we can produce other physiological effects, such as healing. By concentrating on detailed images of healing and health, we can communicate healing states to our bodies.

Not surprisingly, most of the experimental evidence for the physiological effects of immersion comes from studies on visualization and healing. These studies investigate visualization and healing with a range of debilitating disorders, including cancer, heart disease, bone and tissue injuries, infections, and chronic pain. Subjects are taught initially how to immerse themselves in mental imagery and then are monitored before and after treatment.

Training typically involves making detailed mental pictures of the illness and then imagining the illness transformed into a healed outcome.

The majority of these studies show that detailed imagery creates statistically significant improvements in mood, physical effects, and pain perception—including accelerated healing and increased strength and comfort levels. Some of these studies have even shown that mental practice is close to or as good as actual physical practice in the improvement of physiotherapy subjects.

Please note that the techniques described here are not meant to stand in the place of qualified medical advice. The actions needed to move you toward your target state may well include traditional and nontraditional medical care.

The most publicized research on healing and imagery has been conducted by the radiation oncologist Carl Simonton, MD, who is currently the founder and director of the Simonton Cancer Center in Pacific Palisades, California. In his book *Getting Well Again*, Dr. Simonton presents several cases of patients fighting off cancer by visualizing tumors shrinking in vivid detail.

Simonton's patients are initially taught basic body awareness and are then shown how to construct detailed images of the healing process. They may, in particular, be taught to visualize cancer cells as weak and sluggish organisms, such as snails, and their immune cells as strong and aggressive predators, like sharks (and even Pac-Men) that attack and eat up the cancer cells. Afterward, patients are instructed to imagine seeing the cancer cells shrink and be carried away by the body's immune and elimination systems. Finally, the visualization ends with patients imagining they are feeling better and enjoying more energy, a better appetite, and greater zest for life.

A typical visualization session is about fifteen minutes. Each session is then repeated three times a day for a period of several weeks. In many cases, tumor reductions have been verified by biopsies.

Another source of astounding accounts of body effects with detailed imagery is in the area of monks and meditation. One of the most well-known accounts was reported by Dr. Herbert Benson, a cardiologist at the Boston-Henry Institute for Mind Body Medicine in Boston, Massachusetts. Dr. Benson studied Tibetan monks for some time and discovered that these amazing monks could withstand subfreezing temperatures overnight at 15,000-foot elevations in nothing more than sheets simply by visualizing fire brewing and flowing through their bodies.

And there are anecdotal stories to tell as well. About seven years ago, I suffered from persistent chest pains and arrhythmias and did not know why. I calmly focused inward and was directed to a place over my upper right atrium. There I noticed a dark, rigid area. When I went to investigate this with my cardiologist, we discovered the area to be an inflamed sinus node. I began visualizing this area returning to a normal color and texture over the next several weeks. The arrhythmia eventually stopped, and my heart has been fine since.

Another story comes from Rupert, a client of mine who suffered from cervical neck pain after a vehicle accident a few years prior. Once instructed on how to enter a calm inner focus, Rupert went home to imagine a realignment of his discs as well as a decrease in inflammation in the area in order to relieve pressure on the nerves. The next day, he discovered that the pain had significantly decreased, and mobility in his neck had returned for several days after this episode.

Another client, Samantha, was diagnosed with a brain tumor. After hearing the news, she went home to pray and meditate for several weeks. To her surprise, she found that the tumor had disappeared on subsequent medical scans.

These are just a few examples of the power of calm focus on physical health. There are many more that, along with the documented research on mind-body effects, provide ample evidence that a focused mind can produce physiological changes well beyond what is capable in a normal state of mind. To learn how to evoke such healthy states, check out the following exercises.

————

In the next three exercises, we're going to learn how to concentrate awareness on a single target. If you've been practicing the focus control exercises in
previous chapters, you should find it easier to do these exercises. In particular,
you will be able to hold your focus on a target long enough to develop details
about it, as well as immerse yourself in a desired mental and physical state.

Exercise 5.1: Target Detailing

In this exercise, we're going to learn how to concentrate our awareness on
a target and gather information about it. The mind tends to immerse itself
when it actively seeks new information. To ensure we develop the necessary
details, remember to gently return your focus back to the object of interest if
it strays. If you can keep your focused settled in one place long enough, you
should begin to notice a deepening of awareness and a sense of details that
you did not notice before, much like being able to see rocks at the bottom
of a stream once the mud and debris settle.

1. Go to a quiet, comfortable place free of distractions. Remove
   any restrictions and sit in a comfortable, upright position.
   Place your hands on your thighs.

2. Inhale, then slowly exhale as you imagine releasing tension
   through your breath. Relax. Quiet your thoughts.

3. Select a target to focus on, such as a candle flame, photograph,
   or a piece of fruit. Put the object in front of you. Focus on this
   item and nothing else.

4. Describe to yourself the target in detail. Notice its shape,
   size, color, and texture. Note each of its parts.

5. Close your eyes and try to visualize what you have just
   described. Put in as much of the detail as possible.

6. Open your eyes and notice any details you missed. See how much new information you can locate about your target item.

7. Close your eyes again and try to visualize these added details.

8. Shift your focus to your breathing. Follow its rhythm for a minute without altering it. Note the rise and fall of your chest like ocean waves. Note the difference in sensation as air moves in versus when it moves out. See if you can settle your focus enough to tune in to subtle sensations you didn't notice before. Observe for two to five minutes.

9. Open your eyes and return your focus to the room.

Exercise 5.2: Imagery Immersing

In this exercise, we learn how to use imaginary sensory details to create an internal deepening. We'll start with the visual sense and then add the other senses until we create a total immersion in an internal image. This exercise will prepare us for the subsequent exercise, which is designed to evoke a resourceful state.

Enter into a calm focus again and recall or imagine, as much as possible, a sensory experience of the following:

1. **Sight:** Picture a happy scene from your memory. Look around in the scene and note the layout of objects and people in the scene. Describe the scene to yourself. Note its distinctive shapes, colors, and characteristics.

2. **Sound:** Note the sounds of the scene. Listen to the activity in the scene and to any words being said. Note the direction of sounds. Try to hear these sounds in your head.

3. **Taste/Smell:** Pay attention also to any smells or tastes in the scene. You might note the distinctive smell of plants, the

surrounding air, perfumes, or the aroma and/or taste of foods. Smells can be some of our most vivid and deep recollections, so spend time on this sense even if you do not immediately recall tastes or smells in the memory.

4. **Kinesthetic:** Move around in the scene and get a feel of your body in motion. Pay special attention to your reactions to the scene. Note any feelings such as joy, excitement, peace, or relaxation, as well as sensations within your body. Describe these feelings and sensations to yourself.

5. **Intensify the experience:** Note some aspect of the scene that makes you feel especially good and add details to this aspect until it becomes even more vivid. Sit quietly in this scene, immersing yourself in all of its sensory details for about five minutes or as long as you think appropriate.

6. Open your eyes and return to the room.

Exercise 5.3: Evoking a Solution State

In this exercise, we'll practice transforming a problem into a solution state through the use of concentrated immersion. To do this, we identify the problem to be corrected, the state we'd rather have in its place, and the actions needed to create transformation. Then we mentally rehearse these actions in order to ensure that they are automatically triggered when we need them in the real setting.

1. To start, state the problem situation you want changed. Write a brief description of the situation in the space provided at the end of this section. Describe the context: Where are you? When? With whom?

2. Next, narrate the situation as a series of unfolding events (think of frames in a storyboard or comic strip). Starting with the

events just before the trouble begins, unfold the scene until you reach the point of difficulty; this is the place where you first notice the problem arise and performance decline. It is at this point that we will take corrective action.

If you don't know where this sticking point occurs, close your eyes for a moment and imagine the problem situation from start to finish, but from a detached perspective. Do not go into the scene. Stand back and observe what you do in the situation from a distance. Monitor your actions as a dispassionate observer. At what point are you managing? Now, at what point do you start noticing a change? What are the actions that follow? Write these actions down in the space provided.

Example: I am at work during a typical work day. My boss asks to see me in his office. I start to become apprehensive, and my heart starts racing. Next, I enter his office and he begins to talk loudly. At this point, I am so self-conscious that I can't really respond to his questions, so he gets angrier at me.

3. Next, state exactly what you want the situation to be changed into at this point. Include what and how it will be changed and exactly what you will be thinking, feeling, saying, and doing differently in the situation. Be specific about these actions. The more detail you include at this point, the easier it will be to see how to use these actions in your imagination and the more likely they are to manifest in the real setting. Be especially sure to include how positive you will feel in this new state.

Example: At this point in the encounter with my boss, I take a deep breath, release tension, and tell myself, "Stop! I've got this. I'm calm and in control." Then I slowly address each of his questions and assert my needs by requesting that he speak to me in a normal tone and just hear me out. I feel confident.

Situation Narrative:

Solution Outcome:

4. Go to a quiet place free from distractions and get comfortable. Close your eyes and enter into calm focus. Recall that a calm focus enables us to sustain images in the mind longer; by doing so, we can work with these images more effectively and create a greater impact. (See the focus control and imagery immersion exercises earlier in the book.)

5. Once in calm focus, pay attention to your emotion and tension level and make sure you are relaxed throughout your body. If you notice any tension, imagine it releasing like steam off a kettle or loosening like tight rubber bands. As you proceed through the following steps, keep a watch on your tension and concentration levels; if you should notice a change in either, simply release the tension, return to a calm state of mind, and focus back on the mental scene and continue on.

6. Imagine the first scene of the situation. Immerse yourself in the setting. Notice the surrounding detail. Incorporate several

imaginary senses and make it vivid—see the sights and hear the sounds. Include the major features and players in the scene.

7. Next, imagine you are in your body in the scene. Be aware of the feel of your body and remember to monitor your tension level. Play out the scene until you get to the point of difficulty, the place where you experience a decline in your performance.

8. At this point, use the actions you described in your solution narrative. Go through the trouble spot using these actions. Make the scene turn out exactly as you want it. See it transform as if it were happening right at this moment. Include the looks and sounds and especially the feel of it. For instance, feel the movement of your body as you move smoothly and easily through the trouble spot. Pay attention to each action as you do it, and feel it being deeply imprinted in your mind and body. Add enough detail so that you actually start to feel the sensations in your body. Also imagine the emotional state you want. Pay attention to the words you say to yourself—"I am calm and in control"—and really try to capture the feeling of confidence and being in control. Focus on the physical sensation of this confident emotion. What does it feel like? Describe it to yourself. Is it empowering? Soothing? Exhilarating? Savor that feeling to send the signal to your inner mind and body that this is the state you want.

Example: You might see, hear, and feel yourself converse with your boss as you breathe calmly, release tension, talk yourself down, and speak slowly and easily.

By adding these details, your simulated performance starts to approximate the actual performance, and it feels more real to your body; therefore, the imprinting is greater.

9. Capture an image from the scene that best represents this
    solution state; this will be your trigger to produce this state
    anytime you need it. For example, a representative image of
    assertiveness would be standing tall with chin held high. Hold
    the image in mind each time you complete a solution sequence.
    After several repetitions, this image should become paired with
    the solution state and become useful alone as a cue to trigger
    the state when you need it. Also, add a positive affirmation
    or general statement to reinforce the solution state. State the
    affirmation in the present tense. Be clear and concise. You
    may, for example, say, "I am calm and confident in this and
    all situations." As you say this affirmation, concentrate
    intently on your trigger image and the confident feeling
    and nothing else.

Once you've gone through this exercise, go back and start at the beginning—replay the scene. Do this three or four times in order to reinforce
the effect. Recall that repeating mental performance leads to a closer ap-
proximation of actual performance. Mental rehearsal produces small, gradual
changes that prepare us for success. By practicing performance ahead of
time, we have it when we need it in the real setting. Remember: the more
you repeat this exercise, the faster you will produce your desired outcome.

For best results, repeat this exercise two or three times a day for ten to fifteen minutes at a time. You may also repeat this exercise (along with your
affirmation) throughout the day whenever you have idle time.

Don't become disappointed if you have trouble doing this exercise or
seeing results at first. Just as with any skill, it takes time to master.

Exercise 5.4: Evoking a Healthy State

Now let's practice evoking a healthy physical state. Return to the site that drew your attention in Exercise 4.2: Expanding Body Awareness and perform the following:

1. Start by imagining white light cascading down around you and penetrating every cell and tissue of your body. See it concentrate in the affected area, illuminating it brightly. Feel the healing warmth of this highly-charged energy.

2. Next, imagine this white light neutralizing any infection and shrinking swollen tissues like a deflating balloon. See cells reorganizing, connections being rebuilt, and tissues weaving themselves back together. Imagine the area turn from a dark, rough texture to a light, smooth texture and into a strong, pliant, and healthy state. If you have trouble imagining this healing transformation, recall a time when you felt at your best and when this area was healthy.

3. Focus on your body (especially the affected area) and how you want it to feel; describe it to yourself. How does it feel to be well? Include as much detail as possible. For example, see yourself getting around and feel your body moving freely, coursing with energy and vitality and being strong. Also include the emotions of having achieved this healing transformation. Imagine yourself smiling and immerse yourself in the feeling of happiness at being well. (Remember to always end each healing session with the full expression of the healthy state.)

4. To help reinforce the state, use a verbal affirmation with the imagery. For example, you may say, "My heart is now healthy and well." Or you can use a variant of the

affirmation used by the French healer Emile Coue, the
father of autosuggestion, who had much success with
patients using affirmations: "My body is healing within.
Each day, in every way, I am becoming healthier and
healthier." As you say these affirmations, concentrate
intently on the image of perfect health and nothing else.

Afterward, repeat the healing process and affirmation three or four times
to reinforce the effect. Then come back and do the procedure two to three
times a day for ten to fifteen minutes per session (or anytime you have a few
moments to spare). Focus on this regularly for several weeks and you should
begin to see some improvement.

PART THREE

Solution Targeting: A Two-Phase Problem-Solving Strategy

SIX

Overview

In the first two parts of this book, we discussed that a problem tends to arise and persist because of an improper view of it. More exactly, we may say a problem persists because we can't see how to get from our current view of it to our desired view. In this chapter, we'll explore at length how we move from a current view of a problem to a desired target view using cycles of broad-narrow focusing. We call this homing in on the target view *Solution Targeting*. Consider our camera lens analogy again. Just as zooming in and out repeatedly with a camera lens can help us locate a target feature in an overall scene, so too can mentally zooming in and out on a problem help us locate a target solution. That is, when we can see the overall context of a situation, we know better where to focus our efforts to get free from it. This zooming-out-and-in process is illustrated here:

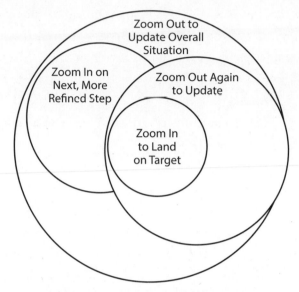

Illustration 6.1: The Solution-Targeting Process

As shown, homing in on a target is not done all at once but in cycles or steps. Steps are easier to attain than a complete solution all at once. Over time, even small steps can lead to big change. Consider how we landed a rocket on the moon—though the rocket was launched thousands of miles from its target, it eventually landed on target by making tiny corrective maneuvers along the way.

We can make such corrective maneuvers to solve our problems as well. For example, in our earlier work-conflict example, I may have expected to be fully confident when talking to my boss after some initial mental practice. However, I will most likely only experience a small change in my behavior, such as a small decrease in tension as I talk to my boss. For this reason, I need to be patient and work to refine my actions over time until I reach my target.

For instance, the first step may have been to take a few deep breaths, place an image of a stop sign before my mind's eye, scan and release body tension, and speak slowly. After testing these actions in the real-life problem setting, I may discover that I need to add self-talk to the mix. If so, the next step would be to mentally practice this self-talk and try it out in the problem setting. Again, after testing, I may discover that this was effective—all I really need to do to remain calm is monitor my tension, speak slowly, and remind myself to stay calm. This would be the third step, and my more refined actions would become my target solution (or target actions). I would then simply continue doing these actions to stay on target.

As another example, if your target is to be happy after being sad for some time, you will have a better chance of reaching this target if you take it in steps. For instance, your first step might be to mentally rehearse getting out of bed and moving about each day. Your second step might be to mentally rehearse making a new friend. Your third step might be to mentally rehearse finding and engaging in a meaningful activity; and so on until you start to feel happy.

In any case, moving from the problem to the target is accomplished by zooming out (mentally broadening our awareness) and zooming in (mentally narrowing our awareness) repeatedly until we land on a target. With each zoom out (which includes looking at the effectiveness of our thoughts and actions), we assess our overall state; with each zoom in, we pinpoint the specific thoughts, actions, or steps that get us closest to our target. Over time, we progressively home in on the few most effective thoughts and actions needed to sustain the target.

Targeting Questions

Solution Targeting is accomplished using three general types of questions: broadening, centering, and narrowing. Each of these questions is used at strategic points to guide the homing process.

Broadening/Observer Mode Questions

Broadening questions help us zoom out and get our overall bearings. Some include: What's really going on here? What am I experiencing right now? Am I where I want to be? If not, where do I want to be? Are these current thoughts and actions getting me there?

Centering Questions

Centering questions help us rein in thought and separate what is central from what is peripheral so we don't get lost in the details. Some of these include: What is holding me up the most in all of this? What factor has the most influence? What am I really trying to accomplish in place of this?

Narrowing/Immersed Mode Questions

Narrowing questions then inquire about the specific thoughts and actions (the details) of what is captured by broadening and centering questions. Some of these include: What thoughts and actions would help get me where I want to be? How would I carry out these thoughts and actions specifically? In what order would I do them?

SEVEN

Zooming Out and Framing Overall Bearings

If you do not change direction,
you may end up where you are heading.
—Lao Tzu

Each cycle of Solution Targeting begins with a zoom out or a step back, which involves broadening into an observer mode and assessing our overall situation.

At times, we may get caught up in life situations and lose ourselves in them; this may be especially true when experiencing high arousal. Zooming out is important at these times because it helps us get out of a narrow view and see alternate options. (See chapter 11: Observing from Broader Mind for an in-depth account of how to recognize and step out of a limited view.)

We assess two things when we zoom out: our current state and our target state. Our current state is our mental-emotional view of a situation at the moment; our target state is the desired condition, free of current limiting thoughts and actions.

For example, if the current problem state is a perceived lack of confidence in social situations, a target state would be access to confident thoughts and actions.

We assess our current state first by observing what we are saying and doing in response to present circumstances; this occurs typically after we notice a change in our emotional-physical state. We may summarize the situation's central factor at this time.

Afterward, we assess the target state. To do this, we may put our current view to a target test, which is a question we pose to ourselves to see if our current state is the target state; this gets us thinking beyond our current circumstances. An example target test would be, "Is this the reaction I want?" If our answer to this question is no, this indicates we have lost ourselves in the current situation and need to acquire a target in order to get out of this limiting state. To do so, we may ask next, "What would be a better reaction? What would be a desirable outcome in place of my current one?"

Troubleshooting the Target

As you can see, locating the target is not always the easiest task. This is especially true if we have been stuck in a problem for some time. After a while, the problem can become such a familiar focus that we come to know more about it than we do about the target solution. The target, or what we want in place of the problem, may seem vague or out of sight.

I see this quite frequently in my practice. From many clients, I hear the common refrain, "I really don't know what I want. I just know I don't like where I'm at." This lack of view other than the problem can keep us stuck. As Henry David Thoreau once said, "People seldom hit what they do not aim at." In fact, they continue to see things in the same fixed way.

For this reason, many of us will frame our target in terms of the current problem. For example, a person may say, "I need to stop being so timid."

However, in doing so, he is still focused on the current problem of timidity. Since we get more of what we focus on, it is best if we focus on something positive we can move toward instead of simply moving away from something negative. We cannot clearly focus on or picture the absence of something. For instance, what actions would "less timid" entail? It would be better to frame the target as "I want to be assertive." Then the man can see the actions needed to produce the desired state—taking a couple of deep breaths, releasing muscle tension, engaging in positive self-talk, speaking slowly and confidently, and so on. This way, the focus is on a positive outcome rather than the removal of a negative one, which will more likely lead the man to the target outcome he seeks.

Often when we have a clear view of where we're going, we can see how to get out of where we are. A specific target often illuminates the steps to getting beyond the problem. Moreover, by focusing on what we want rather than on what we don't want, we have more time to figure out how to get where we want. When the Wright brothers were working out how to fly, they did not focus on how things fell—they focused on how things lifted, such as birds, and then figured out how they could do so.

The same is true of solutions to our problems. When we focus more on what causes the solution rather than on what causes the problem, we have a better chance of finding that solution. For example, we are more likely to overcome a fear of social situations when we focus on actions that lead to confidence than when we spend our time trying to figure out where the fear originally came from. Let the desired target be the yardstick by which you measure and improve your current situation. Study what makes for successes in that area, then repeat or improve on those steps in order to get from your current problem to a solution.

There's an old parable called "Two Frogs in the Milk" that sums up the view that it is better to focus on the desired target than on the current problem. The story goes like this: two frogs fall into a pail of milk. One cries out, "I'm going to drown. I'm going to drown. I'm going to drown." Soon his legs give out and he goes under. The other frog paddles ferociously and shouts, "I've got to get out. I've got to get out. I've got to get out." Surprisingly, he finds himself on a cake of butter he has churned with his furiously moving legs and is able to jump free.

If, like these frogs, you find yourself in a bad situation, be careful about what you focus on because you get more of whatever that is. If you focus on sinking and drowning, that's where you'll go. But, if you keep your focus on finding a way out, you'll keep on kicking and eventually get there.

Often, when clients identify where they would rather be, they find that their lives take on new meaning, and they have the desire and confidence to move forward.

One client, Joan, thought she would never get free of sadness—until she made the concerted effort to spend a few minutes a day envisioning how her life would be if she did not feel the sadness (even though at the time she thought this was an impossibility). Her secret desire—the one she had suppressed for a long time—was to run a flower shop along the beach. She envisioned this desire daily for a few weeks and soon found that she was seizing opportunities and doing small things that moved her closer to this goal; these steps included finding swap meets near the beach and setting up flower stands at them. Shortly afterward, she noticed her sadness lifting and her life looking a little brighter. Today, she is well on her way to building her flower business.

....

Target-Sighting Advantages

A shift to a clear target offers several problem-solving advantages:

- **A Different View to Stimulate New Thoughts and Actions:** A clear target provides the mind a focus other than the problem. A continued focus on the problem is likely to produce more of the same thoughts and reactions that have kept us stuck so far; however, a shift in focus is likely to open new thoughts and actions that can get us moving again.

- **A Guiding Beacon:** A clear target can act as a beacon or reference point that guides us. When we have a destination, we have a better sense of where we're headed and how to get there. We can determine the steps that are needed to get from where we are to where we want to be.

- **A Glimpse of the Finish Line:** A clear target shows us the finish line. With it, we can temporarily transcend the problem long enough to see what things will look like when we are free of the problem; this way, we have a sign or marker that indicates when we're out of the problem. A clear target is like an answer to a math problem at the back of a book—when we know what the final answer looks like, we can work backward to identify the steps needed to reach that answer.

- **A New Horizon:** A clear target draws us in with hope and anticipation for what is to come. Once we have a glimpse of how life can be without a problem, we are inspired to forge ahead despite the current problem. We're not just focused on the awfulness of the problem, we're looking ahead to the future. The more vivid we can make this picture, the more it will inspire us.

....

The key to successfully locating a target solution is to strike a balance between paying attention to the current problem and to the desired target. We shouldn't deny our present circumstances; rather, we accept that we are currently challenged by them and are likely to feel upset. But we include another possibility in our scope as well—this way, we thin out the bad, so to speak, and don't focus on it. Otherwise, the longer we stay solely focused on where we are, the more difficult it will be to shift from it.

In finding a target solution, make sure you've addressed the central factor in the problem and are not looking too soon for a solution. Easy solutions are rarely lasting ones. If you find it difficult to stop talking about the problem even after you've identified a target solution, it is likely you haven't put your finger on the central factor yet. If so, make sure to address the real problem before shifting to the target.

Once you identify the central factor in the problem, shifting your attention to the target can be as easy as shifting the figure and background in the vase/faces illusion. Just like in that illusion (as in all perceptions), we see either one view or another depending on which one we currently put in the foreground as figure and which one we place in the background. We can do the same with our current problem and the desired target. Most of the time, the problem is in the foreground of our lives, so that is all we see. But what would happen if we let it fade into the background for a moment? What would happen if the problem were somehow less of a negative influence? What then would you envision your life being like? What would you imagine doing in place of the problem? What possibilities might come to the foreground?

The key to a successful shift to a target, though, is to stop trying to figure how to solve the problem just yet. We simply let go of the need to do this and assume that we'll find a way as soon as we figure out where we want to go. Some of my clients call this "going on faith." We just keep in mind that we haven't got the answer yet, but we will as soon as we figure out where we're going.

Working backward from the solution to the current problem is a very effective, creative problem-solving technique. Again, it's like getting the answer to a math problem in the back of a book and using the answer to work out the steps. It makes it much easier to solve a problem.

We can start loosening our view of the problem and begin shifting attention to the target by acknowledging the possibility that we might be taking a limited view of our current situation; that is, our current view may be only one of several views available, so we are not going to get too attached to it.

This leaves room for other possibilities. For instance, although we may feel that a problem is insurmountable, we tell ourselves that this is only how it appears at the moment; our view may change later.

The key here is to temporarily let go of what has *been* done and see what *can be* done. We leave options open and don't shut out new ideas too soon. We entertain them. For instance, we don't say, "Things can't change because they have been this way too long." We say instead, "If things could change, what would they be like? And what can I do right now to make this happen? What do I need? Where can I get it?" And then we think about some possibilities.

Bill was convinced that he would never get over the emotional abuse he endured as a child—until he began to learn how to separate himself from his thoughts and recognize them for what they are: current theories of how things are. Once he recognized this separation, he could look at other possibilities. For instance, instead of focusing solely on the notion that the abuse was permanent, he was asked to entertain the possibility that if he did somehow get over it, what would his life look like then? What would he be doing differently? Bill did this and started finding some possibilities.

The most powerful way to shift your attention from a current problem onto a target solution is to explore the opportunity of learning in the problem. When we frame problems solely as impediments, we have trouble seeing them any other way. But when we frame them as opportunities in disguise, we have an avenue or way forward. We can extract the valuable message from the problem that tells us what is needed in the situation to move forward. Look for the silver lining in any situation.

For example, we can frame depression as an obstacle that oppresses us or we can frame it as a signal to ourselves that we need to change something about our life; this may mean getting out more, making new friends, or starting a new career. Likewise, losing a job or relationship may be a difficult loss to get over at first. But we may find it less so when we frame it as an opportunity to find what we're really looking for. If this is the case, it may turn out that losing that job or partner is the best thing that could have happened to us.

Recall that every situation inherently has multiple meanings depending on the perspective we take. In some Eastern philosophies—particularly in Taoism—the world is seen as a balance of opposites. Both good and bad reside in any situation. By keeping our eye on the good, we may transform an obstacle into an opportunity. We may find the meaning in the pain and extract the lesson to be learned. In this way, the pain serves a purpose: it becomes a path to personal and spiritual growth.

Looking for the message in the pain can be especially valuable for those suffering bouts of grief, when it can become extremely difficult to step back and see the loss in any other frame. In fact, no matter what the loss—whether it is the loss of a relationship, job, health, or loved one—we can get through it when we make an effort to find the deeper meaning in it. Don't lose hope; choose to look at it a different way and grow from it.

We can resist the reality before us or we can transform it. If we resist, we don't change the situation and only add to our suffering. However, if we transform the situation, we may not escape it, but at least we don't add to our suffering. It's a matter of taking care of our inner state. We simply decide that no matter what happens, we will not add to our suffering.

I have seen many clients overcome hardships over the years. Most of these people share a few things in common. First, after successfully overcoming a hardship, their priorities tended to change. They started to become more focused on personal and spiritual growth rather than material gain. Second, they tended to seek deeper knowledge and meaning as well as ways to improve themselves. For instance, they often took up new hobbies, went back to school, or changed careers. Third, they began to care more about others. They spent more time with family and friends and often would volunteer to help the less fortunate. And finally, they spent a lot more time looking for the lessons in life's situations.

Stan was emotionally abused as a child. Born of authoritarian parents, he was often punished and criticized for his behaviors, yet given little or no praise for his accomplishments. Later, as Stan became an adult, he sought solitary jobs that allowed him to avoid social interaction. He liked being around people but was afraid of being judged. He came to see me, and we talked about this fear. I asked him what he thought he might have gained from his lifelong struggle with this fear. He was initially taken aback by this question, but after some thoughtful consideration, he replied, "You know, I've always wanted to help others. I guess what I've gained the most from my experience is that I could be very useful to someone else like me. I mean, I've got all the years and skills in dealing with this situation." Now Stan volunteers his time being a big brother to abused children. When asked how things are going now, he said, "Life is easier when you turn your lemons into lemonade."

Take a moment now to ask yourself what challenges you've faced in life. Stay out of the emotion and explore these experiences from a detached perspective. Pick one and ask yourself further, "What did I learn from this situation? How have I made things better or gotten stronger because of it?" Then ask yourself, "What can I do differently now to continue this learning?" Define your thoughts.

······························

SUCCESSFUL PROBLEM SOLVERS AND SOLUTION DETECTION

Observation of those who often solve problems reveals that these people tend to focus not only on the obstacles in a situation but also on potential avenues and exceptions. In addition, they tend to be more optimistic about solving problems—as well as their abilities to do so—and are able to control their thoughts and persist toward a solution.

······························

Framing the Overall Situation

When assessing current and target states, we engage in a process of *framing*. Framing refers to the act of clarifying thoughts so as to get a clear view of the current and target states. Often, as we calmly assess thoughts from broader areas of mind, they enter focal awareness vague and unformed. Framing allows us to affix temporary labels to these impressions in order to make them more tangible and assessable. To do this properly, we need to avoid extraneous detail and use only the most accurate words to capture these impressions.

Our label is only a tentative hypothesis. It must be frequently refined to get a clear view of the situation. To refine, we use calibration questions, so named because they require us to think a little further about the situation, which in turn "calibrates" our view of the situation. For example, we may start with the tentative frame of our current state: "So the main thing here is that I have little say at work?" This is followed by calibration questions: "Is this the problem exactly? Or is there something else at play? What is the main factor? What is causing most of the problem or having the most influence?" A pause at this point allows room for additional thoughts to enter focal awareness and further define the situation: "So the main thing here is not so much that I don't know what to say to my boss but that I have trouble getting my words across."

This calibration continues—tentative proposals followed by a request for clarification—until we capture the right frame. Play like a detective unraveling a mystery, gently probing your broader mind, until you bring a clear picture of the situation into focal awareness. With enough questions, we should be able to expand our view of the situation enough to see both the current and the target states. The process is similar to zooming out of a scene with a camera and aligning the scene's major features in the camera's frame. In this way, our initial probe turns into a highly accurate reading of the situation.

Framing, though, requires a bit of patience and flexibility. On one hand, we need to be open to the flow of thoughts entering from our inner mind; on the other hand, we need to be on the lookout for a specific label for these thoughts. In order to do this, we perform framing in the zone of optimal performance. Recall that in this zone, we have moderate levels of arousal and a more free control over our focus. We can shift easily between opening to all thoughts and closing in on a particular thought.

Framing Questions

Below are a series of questions you can ask your inner mind in order to frame both your current and target states. Ask first about the current state and then the target state. Typically, we begin to ask about the current state when we first notice a change in our emotional-physical state. You may use the following broadening/observing questions:

- What am I experiencing right now?

- Is this the experience or reaction I want?

- If not, what are the major factors creating or sustaining this experience?

Afterward, pause to gather your thoughts and then home in on the central factor using a few centering questions, such as

- Of the things that came forward, what factor is holding me up and having the most influence in all of this?

- What factor is the common connection to all these other factors?

These questions are then followed with an assessment of the target state. The target state is framed using a combination of broadening and centering questions:

- Now that I know what the real problem is, what can I learn from this awareness to move forward?

- How can I turn the problem into an opportunity or a chance for growth?

- What other ways can I see things?

- What is most needed in this situation?

- What can I shoot for as a result of this learning?

- What is a desirable outcome in place of my
  current situation?

Follow-up calibration questions are also included to get clarification on any broadening or centering question:

- Is this it exactly?

- Is there something else at work here?

- What is the main issue *exactly*?

- What words would capture it just right?

Together, these questions should lead you to a complete picture of where you are and where you wish to go. If you lose your way at any time, remember to refocus using a broadening or centering question, such as:

- What is bothering me the most about all of this?

- What is having the most influence?

- What is needed most in place of this?

Example Framing Dialogue

A simulated dialogue is presented below to illustrate the framing process. In this example, Jim is experiencing a negative emotion and begins to reflect on it.

Surface Assessment: This feeling keeps nagging me. Let me stop for a moment and observe it. What could be causing this feeling? What could be the main factors? [After initial focus opening, Jim sits quietly and observes his thoughts. In the process, he mulls over the major factors in his current situation.]

Inner Response: There's a lot going on lately … For one, I've been tired … don't feel like doing anything … my sleep is bad … been a bit lonely lately but busy at work … and although I don't particularly love my job, it does pay the bills. I am stressed about the bills though. These seem like the major things. [At this point, Jim summarizes what he feels are the major factors.]

Surface Assessment: Okay, so the main things here are poor sleep, fatigue, lost interest, some loneliness, and bills. When I look at all these factors, what do I think is having the most impact on me? What is really bothering me the most?

Inner Response: Mmm … Finances are always a big stressor but … [pauses to access a deeper response] … I guess it's this loneliness that is really affecting me the most. I still miss her. [Jim captures the central factor— grief from losing his girlfriend—and attempts to frame it.]

Surface Assessment: So it would appear that the main thing here is that I am still not over Jill, and this loss is affecting other areas of my life. Is this it exactly?

Inner Response: Yes, this seems to be it. I realize now that I really do care for her, but now I have to accept that she is with someone else.

Surface Assessment: Right now it seems difficult to see how my life will be different than its current negative state without her. [Emphasizing the problem's temporary nature.] But, if I did somehow get past this feeling, what do I think I would be doing then? How would my life be different? [Shifting focus to a possible target.]

Inner Response: Mmm … It's hard to think ahead right now. I just know I can't shake this feeling right now. [Realizing that he is ahead of himself, Jim resorts back to defining the problem.]

Surface Assessment: Let me so slow down a bit and ask myself: What's the worst part of all of this?

Inner Response: Knowing that if I had believed that she could really love me, I would have let her in more and not sabotaged the relationship.

Surface Assessment: So believing and opening up is something I've learned from this experience. What else does this experience tell me about what I need right now to move forward in my life? [Refocusing on the target.]

Inner Response: It's telling me that I have to start doing something about why I believe I can't be loved [addressing core belief].

Surface Assessment: What needs the most attention right now? [Pauses and remains open...]

Inner Response: These critical words that keep popping into my head, like "I'm not good enough, so why should anyone want me?" This is the reason I always sabotage my relationships... because I keep believing and acting on these words.

Surface Assessment: So what I'm really seeking is self-acceptance.

Inner Response: Yes, that feels right. [Target acquired.]

Exercise 7.1: Framing Overall Bearings

This exercise shows you how to size up a situation and get your overall bearings. You can take any situation and step back to see where you are and where you need to go; this is preferable to getting caught up in the confusion. Zooming out opens up new ideas and actions.

1. Choose a situation that has been bothering you lately and then go into calm focus and ask yourself, "What is the main thing bothering me about this? What is holding me up the most?" Calmly think about it and let your thoughts come freely.

2. When a thought comes to mind, don't get caught up in it. Simply ask, "Is this it exactly? Is this the answer? Or is there something else?" Be patient and wait for the best answer. Usually, it takes several guesses.

3. To help find the best answer, make a mental note of the closest guesses and summarize them as a whole. What common theme do they point to? Sum it up in one sentence. This is the frame for the current state.

Guesses:

Summary Frame of the Current State:

4. Next, ask yourself the following target questions and give careful consideration to your responses: Now that I know this, what can I learn from this awareness to move forward? What is needed most now in this situation?

5. Again, when a thought comes to mind, don't get caught up in it. Simply ask, "Is this it exactly? Or is there something else?" Wait until you get an adequate amount of responses and/or you feel you have found the best response, and then summarize the common theme among the best responses; this is the frame for the target state.

Guesses:

Summary Frame of the Target State:

6. Look back on your earlier perception of the problem. What new information have you discovered? What options or directions do you now have that you did not before?

As you can see, zooming out is a valuable tool because it allows us to put things into perspective and determine what is relevant to focus on. By doing this exercise any time you need it, you will avoid scattering your efforts, be able to get your overall bearings, and put your focus where it counts.

EIGHT

Zooming In On the Target Solution

*Any man who can drive safely while kissing a pretty girl is
simply not giving the kiss the attention it deserves.*
—Albert Einstein, attributed

After we have zoomed out and framed our target, we move into the second
phase of Solution Targeting, called *zooming in*. In this phase, we shift from
the detached observer mode into the active immersed mode and examine
the target in detail. Target detail includes the specific thoughts and actions
that best comprise the target state and show us how to do the target.

Fleshing out—or resolving—the target involves answering the following questions:

- What does the target state look like?

- What are the markers or signs that indicate I am on target?

- What small step can be taken now to get closer to this target?

Identifying Target Markers

We seek to resolve the target because too often when we first frame a target, our view of it is broad and vague. We may say that what is needed most in a current problem is *peace* or *happiness*. But such abstract views of a target state offer little information on how we may reach that state.

By identifying and immersing ourselves in the thoughts and actions that make up the target state, we can in effect produce this state. Recall that most target states consist of a sequence of thoughts and actions that actually evoke the state. For example, the vague target state of *peace* is much easier to capture when one resolves and performs its individual actions of taking a couple of deep breaths, monitoring and releasing tension, and telling oneself, "I am calm."

We call these individual actions that make up the target state *target actions* or *target markers* since they both produce and indicate the presence of the target. By clarifying them, we can see specifically how to do the target and what the signs will be when we reach our goal. The more specific we can be with these thoughts and actions, the better.

All we have to do after identifying target markers is mentally immerse ourselves in these thoughts and actions and practice them. Then we test them in the problem setting. The feedback we get from the road test will tell us how close we came to producing the target state and what else is needed (our next step) to reach our target. (See Exercise 5.3: Evoking a Solution State for a detailed explanation of this mental practice.)

Target-Resolving Questions

To resolve target actions, we ask the following open questions:

- Now that I know what is needed (e.g., I have my target state of calm assertiveness in mind), how would I define this state?

- What are its main features?

- What thoughts and actions does it involve specifically?

- If I were on target right now (e.g., calmly assertive), what would I be thinking and doing differently that I am not doing right now?

- Additionally: How will I know when I reach this target? What are the most distinctive actions to look for?

Shifting Perception to Identify Actions

One way we can improve target resolving is by imagining we are observing ourselves perform the target on a TV screen. Doing this requires that we shift our focus to an outside observer mode, where we are in a better position to see the individual actions involved. We call this detached description of observed actions *target picturing*. Some questions that put us in this observer mode are:

- If I were watching myself perform the target (e.g., being calmly assertive) on a TV screen, what actions would I see myself doing to maintain this desired state despite the difficulty?

- What actions would I be doing first? Second? Third? Then what?

Then we can imagine that we are entering into the screen and mentally playing out these actions as if it they were happening in real time. Doing this immerses us in the target state and reinforces or imprints it on a deeper level; this way, the target state is more likely to manifest when we need it in the actual problem setting. (Again, see Exercise 5.3: Evoking a Solution State for a detailed explanation of mental rehearsal.)

Recalling Successful Times to Identify Actions

Another useful strategy for identifying target actions is to use examples from the past or other contexts in which we or someone we observed approximated this solution target.

Situations don't stay the same, so there are always times when we or someone else acted on target, or at least came close to it. For example, if we think about it, we may recall times when we or someone we observed performed actions that produced a state of calm assertiveness during a stressful event, or at least a state of lowered anxiety. We call these models or examples of target behavior *target times*. They can be valuable resources for locating present target actions. We simply think about these times and see what actions we might borrow from them to produce the present target state.

If, for example, your target is to be calm, you might explore the times you calmed yourself down during difficult times and then see what you might use now to calm yourself. To identify the key actions you used in that past situation, simply compare what you were thinking, saying to yourself, and doing during these target times. Ask yourself, "What did I say to myself and do at this successful time that I'm not saying or doing now?"

Some target time questions include:

- What steps have I taken so far to get me closer to my target?

- When did I come close to this goal in the past during a difficult time, even if only a little bit?

- If I can't find any steps to get closer, what have I done to maintain my current position? How have I kept myself from getting further away from my target, even despite the difficulty?

- How did I do them even though things were so difficult?

- What did I think, say to myself, or do during that past success that I'm not doing now?

- What was most helpful or useful about what I did? What actions seemed most effective?

- How did these thoughts and actions help me exactly?

- Which ones seem easy enough to sustain on a regular basis?

Although it can be useful to model your actions after someone else's successful behavior, you'll likely get more results reusing your own behaviors. This is so for several reasons: One, our own actions have proven to work with us before, and odds are that they will work for us again. Two, they're familiar and therefore easier to do than learning new actions. Three, they tend to evoke the resourceful state we were in before, helping us to temporarily transcend the negative feelings associated with the current problem long enough to experience the confident feeling of success; this reacquired feeling is likely to reinvigorate us to go out and actively seek our target state.

Noting the Distinctions

Still another way we can help identify target actions is to include distinctions in our questions, such as "How did I get one step closer to the target, *despite the difficulty, if only a little bit.*" The qualifier "despite the difficulty, if only a little bit" keenly focuses us on looking for *any* action, no matter how small, as long as it addresses the obstacle before us. In addition, qualifiers like *specifically* and *exactly*, as in "How did I do this *exactly*? What *specific* actions were involved?" ensure that we locate the details of these actions.

For many of my clients who have trouble seeing a way out of their difficulties, these simple maneuvers help them identify the details of what they can do and encourage them to forge ahead. Plus, these techniques offer clients hope that there is something they can do today. Even small actions can help us feel more powerful and in control of problem situations.

Pinpointing the Next Step

The last stage of zooming in and resolving target actions is to find the next step toward the target. Recall that most often we are not going to reach our target all at once. We will have to reach it in stages. Identifying the next step forward ensures that we continue to move closer to our target and that we will eventually reach it.

Fortunately, all we need to do to find the next step toward a target state is find an effective action. Often, we think it takes a lot of effort to produce a target state, so we either scatter our effort or avoid any effort. But all we really need to do is be selective and find those few actions that can make the difference. When we do, we concentrate our effectiveness like a laser beam.

In fact, no action is insignificant—no matter how small—if it starts linking our current state with the target state. Even an action as small as telling oneself, "I have someplace to go today," may spark hope and a desire to get out of bed, which may in time lead to greater happiness. Thus, small acts can make a large difference if you follow through on them.

Next Step Questions

Finding the next step to a target can be made easier by asking ourselves the following next-step questions:

- What can I learn from my progress so far?

- Knowing this, what's my next step? What actions can I do right now to get closer to my target, if only a little bit?

- What specific thoughts and actions can I do?

- Where in my current situation can I begin to use these actions?

Using a Scale to Find the Next Step

We can also find our next step toward a target by using a numbered 1–10 scale. A numbered scale allows us to gauge our progress toward the target in an incremental way.

To construct a target positioning scale, imagine a dart board with ten concentric rings, numbered from 1 at the outer ring to 10 at the center bull's-eye. Ring 1 represents the furthest we have ever been from our target, 10 represents the attainment of our target, and the rings in between represent intermediate steps.

Start to gauge your position relative to the target by choosing the number on the scale that best represents where you think you are at this moment. What number would you pick to represent where you are right now in relation to this target? To find the next step, ask yourself what small action would get you one point closer to the target.

If you have trouble identifying this next step, you could do several things. One is to recall a target time and reuse the actions from this time to identify a step closer. You may ask, "What number have I been at when I am closest to my target? How did I get there? What specific thoughts and actions did I do? Knowing this, what can I do now to move one point closer or even just half a point closer?"

Yet another way to find the next step is to project your position one step closer on the scale and ask how you reached this step. "I'm currently at 3. If I moved to 4, what would I imagine I would be thinking and doing that I'm not doing now? How did I get to 4?"

Scaling can be used to measure a variety of factors besides target closeness, including mood, hope, confidence, and motivation. In particular, scaling such things as motivation and confidence may clarify or quantify exactly where you stand emotionally in regard to a target goal. Example: "On a scale of 1 to 10, where 1 stands for the furthest I have been from having sufficient confidence in reaching my target, and 10 represents the closest, what number would I choose to represent where I am right now in degree of confidence? What would get me one point closer in confidence? Suppose I did get one point closer, what would change for me? What would I think and do then?"

Target-Resolving Dialogue

In the last chapter, we presented the case of Jim to illustrate how we go about getting our overall bearings on a problem. Recall in that example that Jim had framed the target solution to his current problem (sadness) as a need for self-acceptance. According to Jim, a belief that he is not good enough led him to sabotage his last relationship (as well as previous ones). We enter now with a continuation of his inner dialogue as Jim begins to resolve the target solution:

Surface Assessment: What makes someone truly good enough? What are the main features of self-acceptance?

Inner Response: I guess being comfortable in one's own skin, being real about one's strengths and weaknesses, and being kind to oneself.

Surface Assessment: What would it feel like to express these features for just a moment? After all, I can do anything in my imagination. What do I think I might say to myself and do that is different than what I do right now? [Attempting to resolve the target.]

Inner Response: I guess I would feel that I deserve to have someone in my life, and I would be more confident in getting that person.

Surface Assessment: What exactly would I be thinking and doing? [Developing further action detail.]

Inner Response: I probably would be telling myself I'm good enough, and not comparing myself to others, because I'd realize that we're all the same deep down; and so, I probably would be dating more. But I don't see how I am going to be doing this.

Surface Assessment: There's that negative thinking again. [Separating from the thoughts.] Let's just say that presently I cannot see how I am going to get there; this is only how I see it at the moment. My view could change. Let me think—when was there a time when I could have been down on myself, but I didn't compare myself with others, and so felt comfortable being me?

Inner Response: Mmm … I'm not sure there is a time. I can't recall right now.

Surface Assessment: Let me just relax for a moment and give myself time to explore my thoughts. [Entering further into a calm focus.]

Inner Response: Oh yeah, when I was in sixth grade, I won the science fair even though I thought at first I wasn't good enough. There were many projects better than mine, and I was really scared about even entering the contest.

Surface Assessment: What did I tell myself at this time that convinced me to enter even though at first I thought I wasn't good enough? What made the difference?

Inner Response: I just said to myself, "What's the problem? If I don't win, I'll still enjoy talking about my project."

Surface Assessment: So, at that point, I wasn't comparing myself to others. I was more focused on what I created, and so I could be myself and express freely. Is that it exactly? Or is it something else?

Inner Response: Yeah … that's it. It didn't matter anymore. I stopped focusing on thoughts about me and took my ego out of the equation; therefore, I could be my real self.

Surface Assessment: What if I were to try this same strategy in my current situation? I say to myself, "Although I have thoughts that I'm not good enough, it doesn't matter. I'm still going to remind myself that we're all the same deep down and each of us has something to offer. Therefore, I can be myself and feel good about it."

Inner Response: I guess that feels all right.

As you can see, Jim was able to frame the problem, sight the solution, and resolve the solution in a fairly short period of time simply by using the Solution-Targeting process. As a result, he now has a specific action plan for overcoming the problem. He can repeatedly remind himself that we all are unique, we all matter, and he can express himself freely as he takes some time to let this new script become familiar until it eventually overrides the old script.

Exercise 8.1: Resolving the Target

This exercise shows you how to resolve an identified target through the use of open questions. To start, take the frame of the target identified in Exercise 7.1: Framing Overall Bearings, and ask yourself the following questions:

1. When have I come closest to reaching this target in the past?

2. If I can't find such a time, when did I at least come close to reaching something like it?

3. What did I think and do that is different from what I normally do?

4. How can I use these thoughts and actions now to make things better?

Again, allow your thoughts to flow freely, and summarize your findings. By the time you're done asking these questions, you should have a better idea of what you can do to move from the current problem toward the desired target state. All of these questions help you to focus and resolve action details. They help pinpoint the most effective actions needed to move you forward and prevent scattering and diffusing your effort.

NINE

Landing and Staying On Target

To map out a course of action and follow it to an end requires
some of the same courage which a soldier needs.
—Ralph Waldo Emerson

Solution Targeting—broad and narrow cycles of assessing and pinpointing actions—continues until we land on a target or at least reach a place where we feel satisfied with our progress toward a target state. In the latter case, the problem may still remain, but we have enough of what we're looking for that the problem doesn't seem like much of a problem anymore.

In either case, we may decide to stay the course and maintain our position using the effective actions we've identified so far, or we may decide to shoot for a new target. If we shoot for a new target, we begin a new cycle of Solution Targeting in a new direction. For instance, after seeing that we can be calm and confident with our boss, we may decide that we really do have the confidence to go out and get what we want. If so, our target may change to obtaining a new job.

Reaching a satisfactory position, however, depends on the length and severity of the problem and on our focusing skill. With problems that are sufficiently long or intense, there is usually a sizeable imprinting of the problem pattern. Mental and physical habits can become ingrained.

Getting beyond the problem under these circumstances will require sufficient skill at mentally practicing target behavior, which should be done in great detail and over time. If so, target behavior will imprint and eventually replace problem behavior.

Ongoing Target Monitoring

Once we reach a target state, though, we don't stop. We should maintain a good habit of monitoring our current and target positions on a regular basis. The problem we worked so hard to overcome is still familiar territory—if we're not observant, we're bound to slide back into it as well as its ineffective thoughts and actions.

To help us stay observant, we may use a *target chart*, which is a simple log for monitoring our ongoing progress. Here is an example of a target chart I use in my practice. You can re-create it or even photocopy copies of it for your own use. With it, you can stay out of autofocus longer and be more aware of your target state and on- and off-target behaviors. We will talk more about how to stay in the observing, monitoring mode in chapter 11: Observing from Broader Mind.

TARGET:				
Date and time	Feeling description (good, bad, happy, sad, etc.)	Target closeness (10=on target, 1=off target)	Situation and context (what, where, with whom?)	Associated thoughts and actions before and during the situation

Illustration 9.1: Target Chart

At the top of the chart, write a brief description of your target as it currently stands for the week. Next, pay attention to your feelings each day. When you notice a change in feeling regarding your goal, record it. In the first two columns, write the date and time the feeling occurred and a descriptive word about the feeling. In the third column, scale how close you feel at the moment to your target using the 1–10 measure discussed earlier. Finally, in the last columns, provide a brief description of the situation in which the feeling occurred (include what happened, where, and with whom) as well as your thoughts and actions before and during the situation.

After a week or so of recording your feelings about a certain goal, look for patterns. Compare the times when you seemed closer to your target goal with the times you felt further from it, and note what you were thinking and doing in both cases. Then make a new target to stop doing what was getting you further from your overall goal and do more of what was getting you closer to it. Think more about what you can add to these on-target behaviors to get you even closer to your overall goal.

Many clients report that keeping a target chart helps increase their awareness of what they want and what they are thinking and doing each week in order to achieve those goals. Target charting has not only significantly improved their ability to reach their targets but also their overall mood, confidence, and relationships.

PART FOUR

*Accessing
Broader
Mind*

TEN

Harvesting Solutions from Broader Mind

If I were to try to put words to the essential truth revealed by the mystic experience, it would be that our minds are not apart from the world; and the feelings we have... are not of ourselves alone, but are glimpses of a reality transcending the narrow limits of our particular consciousness.
—Sir Arthur Eddington, astrophysicist

So far, we have discussed how our inner mind can be harnessed to solve problems. We've seen how insights can be extracted with open questions and how solution outcomes can be manifested by delivering detailed imagery to our inner mind.

In this chapter, we explore the possibility of harnessing deeper, broader areas of mind. Recall our discussion of the layers of mind in chapter 4. In that discussion, we presented an analogy of a spotlight to represent these layers of mind. Refer back to the illustration on page 48: the bright center represented our focal awareness or conscious mind and the outer, shaded areas represented entry into the subconscious mind. We can modify that analogy now to represent the relationship of our conscious mind to our subconscious mind and to the deepest, broadest area of mind: the *universal mind*.

We have discussed the conscious and subconscious minds already. Recall that the conscious mind comprises the smallest area of our total mind. Its main function is to filter much of the information that reaches our awareness so we may attend to immediate concerns without being overloading with information. The conscious mind is the part of us that we identify as the self, or *I*. It is the part that is self-aware. It is our focal awareness.

Again, just outside the conscious mind is the region of the personal subconscious mind. This area of mind is larger than the conscious mind and stores all our life's memories, motor skills, habits, and automatic programs. Information is kept here as backup so that the conscious mind is free to attend to immediate concerns and can access this information when needed. Most of what we do each day—such as drive a car or brush our teeth—is on subconscious automatic programming. Once we learn a task, it is relegated to the subconscious, and we no longer have to attend to every aspect of it consciously.

In fact, much of the information the mind takes in and processes is outside conscious awareness. The subconscious processes a multitude of data about the environment and internal physiological states every single moment and keeps up with all the vital functions of the body, including heart rate, breathing, metabolism, body temperature, and digestion—all without conscious control.

It even works while the conscious mind is asleep. If we have a problem, it will ruminate on all the factors involved and synthesize a solution while the conscious mind rests. This solution will be delivered to the conscious mind when it is ready.

Last but not least, the universal mind is the largest area of mind and extends beyond the personal mind to include all minds—and quite possibly the universe itself. It is the underlying consciousness that we all share and the storehouse where all the experiences of the universe are kept, including the knowledge of billions of years of physical and biological evolution and the experiences of all sentient beings who ever lived. The Swiss psychologist Carl Jung called this broadest, deepest mind the "collective unconscious."

Think of this part of the mind as the Internet and each individual mind as a personal computer. With the right access, we can connect with this vast storehouse of information and possibly receive or transmit any bit of information we desire. It is the home of our brightest and most original ideas and our ability to manifest outcomes. By accessing it, we may gather wisdom, make more-informed decisions, perform at peak ability, and really make things happen. This area of mind can produce some of the most profound solutions to problems.

The Quantum Connection

You may ask, "Can there really be a connection to the universe deep within all of us?! And can we actually harness this connection to solve problems?" Some might think a universal connection is a silly and unlikely notion. But research in quantum physics indicates otherwise. Bear with me here for a slightly technical explanation of just how that occurs.

For nearly a century, scientists have been probing the quantum world— the world of the very small—and have uncovered some astounding things about the nature of reality. One of the most amazing things they have discovered is that at its tiniest level, the universe is not really solid but actually immaterial waves of energy. And these waves connect the universe beyond normal space and time.

That's right. At its tiniest and most basic, the universe is nothing more than energy. In fact, quantum physicists can only explain the physical universe at its tiniest in terms of mathematical relationships and processes—not in terms of the discrete or substantial. We see this in Albert Einstein's famous $E=MC^2$ equation—which shows matter and energy as essentially the same— as well as in the mathematics of other pioneers of quantum physics. For example, Louis de Broglie expressed matter in terms of wavelengths and called all matter, "matter waves." Similarly, Erwin Schrödinger represented all matter as wave functions or spread-out probabilities.

The reality is that the physical world is an illusion. We see the world of objects simply because tiny *vortices* of energy are bound together by forces that give the illusion of solid matter. In actuality, these tiny vortices we call subatomic particles (such as electrons) that make up atoms and the rest of the physical world have a dual nature. They can be both spread-out waves of energy or discrete packets of energy, and they are named particle-waves because of this dual nature. When particle-waves appear as particles, they have a point location in our normal space-time; when particle-waves act as spread-out waves, the particle aspect disappears into the vacuum of space and is not present in normal space-time. At this point, the particle exists only in potential in what is known as a state of *superposition*, or all-possibility.

Moreover, particle-waves have a peculiar way of linking themselves beyond the normal constraints of time and space—so much so that once two or more particle-waves interact, they can forever influence each other no matter how far away they are; they can be light-years or eons apart. For instance, a scientist can change the spin of an electron, and its entangled twin kilometers away may start spinning in the opposite direction. Einstein was so disturbed by this odd phenomenon when it was first discovered in the early 1900s that he called it "spooky action at a distance." Since then the phenomenon has been thoroughly investigated and is well established. Today, we know it as *quantum entanglement,* or nonlocal connection.

So what could be connecting particle-waves and therefore the whole universe at the quantum level? Some scientists have proposed that the wave aspects of particle-waves exist on a deeper dimension and are sharing information in a unified field of information. David Bohm, a physicist and colleague of Einstein, called this deeper dimension the *implicate order*. Others call it the *unified field*, the *zero-point field*, or simply the *quantum vacuum*. Pervading all of space, this underlying field generates an enormous amount of background energy—even in the deepest vacuums of space—and as such, it is thought to be the wellspring of all energy and matter in the universe.

Particle-waves are thought to be generated by the field as pressure waves in its vacuum. Once generated, waves then radiate from the field and collide with each other, much like water ripples collide with each other on the surface of a pond. When they do, they become phase entangled and share information, creating a continuous medium. Thus, they can potentially share information about any and every aspect of the universe and therefore provide a continuous, nonlocal connection across the universe.

Particle-waves share information through their resonance. When two or more frequency waves are in phase or resonate with each other, they become linked as one. For example, we see this when two radio waves or cell phones are in sync—they connect. Thus, as quantum waves collide, they create more complex wave patterns that link information about each individual wave.

With each continued wave interaction, the entire universe becomes built of wave combinations—both simple and complex—whose frequency waves link information about everything in the universe. Over time, as waves progressively entangle with each other, they produce more stable and complex wave systems; this progressive entanglement is the reason large-scale matter behaves as steady-state objects, unlike the apparently random and uncertain behavior of discrete quantum particles.

David Bohm offered the analogy of a hologram to explain how quantum wave patterns could explain the overall interconnectedness of the universe as well as particle formation in three-dimensional space. A *hologram* is a three-dimensional image that emerges from shining light through wave patterns on a two-dimensional photographic plate (e.g., picture light shining through interacting pond ripples). Our three-dimensional universe may arise from the unified field in a similar way. That is, as field forces are guided by quantum wave patterns imprinted in the field, they may create natural holograms in three-dimensional space. We see similar three-dimensional field effects when we observe iron filings aligning along the force lines of a magnetic field.

According to Bohm, quantum waves represent a deeper order that are implicate or non-apparent until they become explicate or manifest as three-dimensional, physical objects. That is, each three-dimensional object in nature has its own two-dimensional wave pattern characterizing it. Wave patterns hold information about objects, in their frequency contrasts, much like contrasts in light waves hold information about a visual object, such as the object's size, shape, color, and texture (as we see in holograms). From this wave information, field forces then guide particle formation in three-dimensional space.

In addition, Bohm saw the universe not as static, but as evolving like a flowing hologram that becomes more intricate and interconnected over time. This seems plausible when we consider the possibility that, within the vacuum of the unified field, there may be nothing to cancel out existing wave patterns except newly-imprinted wave patterns. If patterns are retained in the unified field indefinitely, then the field may contain a certain degree of memory as well as a mechanism for the accumulation of stable, refined patterns over time. In time, these more intricate patterns could become the informational blueprints for more advanced structures such as atoms, molecules, and larger objects. Though physical forms (particle formations) may come and go, deeper wave information is always accumulating and refining subsequent forms.

Again, this progressive entanglement and refinement of particle-waves (which some scientists call *decoherence*) and the field imposing overall order (which Bohm called *quantum potential*) may account for the orderly and steady-state behavior of large-scale matter versus the apparently random and chaotic behavior of individual quantum particles.

Bohm's holographic principles were first introduced in 1952 and later culminated in his 1981 book, *Wholeness and the Implicate Order,* and his 1993 book, *The Undivided Universe.* Today, a number of scientists are coming to agree with Bohm and hypothesize that the universe may in fact work like a giant hologram, with the physical universe being a three-dimensional expression of two-dimensional information stored in a deeper dimension.

Ultimately, at its tiniest level, the universe may not be made of anything solid at all; it really operates as an energy and information construct that gives the *illusion* of a three-dimensional, solid reality. Beneath it all, everything in the universe—including you and me, rocks and trees, electromagnetic and gravity fields, empty space, and even our thoughts—is simply organized patterns of energy and information projected from a deeper field of unified information existing outside this space-time. We might see ourselves and everything as separate, but we may all be connected deep down and continually broadcasting our existence to each other through the energy patterns we are made of. We may influence each other even when we are far apart.

An Evolving, Interconnected Universe

Now, there are several assumptions we can make about the overall state of the universe when we consider this quantum interconnectedness. For one, **we might deduce that the universe operates as a unified whole**. That is, as each part of the universe influences and is influenced by every other part, grand order and symmetry arise. We need only look at the natural world and the exquisite symmetry of galaxies and celestial bodies—as well as the patterns in some life forms, such as the Fibonacci curve found in both romanesco and snail shells—to confirm this hypothesis.

Two, as wave interaction and entanglement continue over time, we may assume that the universe has been gathering and integrating more and more information; and in doing so, **it appears to be "learning" from these interactions, evolving itself over time.** This is evidenced by the enormous complexity of living organisms and ecosystems now populating our world.

Third, **we might assume the presence of intelligence**. That is, if universal order arose from interaction and fine-tuning over time, then the next logical step would be to conclude that a type of systems intelligence emerged. In this case, God would be the collective intelligence of the universe—the intelligence that has been unfolding in this space-time. Think about it: How is a flow of energy and information all that different from a flow of thoughts? When we consider a mind in general, it is simply the movement and interaction of thoughts. How much of a stretch is it to think that a *universal mind* might arise as a result of radiating waves sharing information across the universe?

And finally, as a result of this quantum interconnectedness, **we might deduce our part in the grand scheme of things**. Specifically, since we, like everything else in the universe, are made of quantum waves of information, including our brains and minds, we must therefore be mentally connected to the rest of the universe. As such, it seems plausible that we could both receive and transmit information to the universe as well as influence and be influenced by it. As an example, we may harvest insights from its fertile field and plant our own seeds of thought into it. This sending and receiving of thoughts is what we'll explore next.

Thought Reception

Is it possible to receive "thoughts" from the universe at large? After all, waves of information are interacting throughout the universe all the time. Could it be possible that if we focused calmly, we might intercept some of this universal knowledge? In this case, our brains would be acting as receiving stations for wave information, gathering data and interpreting it into meaningful patterns. By quieting the mental noise and listening to the background, we may directly experience the wider, unified field and attain pure, expanded awareness. Here, universal information would be seeping into focal awareness from broader areas of the mind as our mental filter relaxes. Might this be the source of our original insights, intuitions, and spiritual guidance? Since this information is coming from sources not gained by the local senses, we call it *nonlocal information*.

An Awakening: Making Contact with Universal Intelligence

A sometimes surprising feature of tuning into broader areas of mind is an *awakening,* or a transcendent experience. This type of experience involves a significant insight or revelation and often occurs while in a deep, relaxed state of mind, presumably when one's mental filter is most open.

According to the nineteenth-century psychiatrist and mystic Richard Maurice Bucke, MD, an awakening is the result of making contact with the universe. In his 1901 book, *Cosmic Consciousness: A Study in the Evolution of the Human Mind,* Bucke referred to an awakening as a feature of *cosmic consciousness*—reaching a transcendent state. According to Bucke, when one attains cosmic consciousness, "there is presented to consciousness a clear conception in outline of the meaning and drift of the universe." The experience is usually accompanied by a flash of insight along with feelings of peace, joy, and connectedness.

Bucke believed that Jesus and Buddha (among other notable mental and spiritual leaders) were some of the gifted individuals who could easily connect with this universal consciousness and derive its wisdom. He felt also that these cosmic awakenings provided the impetus and insight for many of the major religions and wisdom traditions throughout history.

A typical awakening, as reported by several of my clients, usually begins with a significant change in mood and sensory experience. One may report an initial feeling of aliveness soon followed by a notable increase in light level and a growing sense of peace or joy. Time seems to stand still and there is a sense of being enveloped by a larger presence and/or feelings of love. At this point, one often receives the insight or revelation.

In reporting her awakening experience, one client reported, "Everything seemed to stand still and I was not conscious of time. Nothing existed but quiet fulfillment. I had no worry, fear, or apprehension. It was just total peace. It felt as if I awoke from a dream and everything made sense for the first time. I could see clearly now what I needed to do."

Words often fail to adequately describe an awakening experience because it transcends normal experience. These short bits of transcendence tend to be so pronounced and life-changing that several of my clients have said that they are the best moments of their lives.

We all have the potential to make contact with this larger intelligence and experience an awakening. It is just that few of us are even aware of our connection. The reason: we are cut off. Too often, we spend our time in a relatively narrow range of awareness focused exclusively on our busy external lives. As a result, we filter out much of the awareness around and in us, except for an occasional spot of intuition or insight. What is needed is to spend a little more time in deep meditation, prayer, or self-reflection. If so, we just may find more than we realized, including some of the answers to our most pressing problems. We will explore how to connect and derive wisdom and guidance from this universal intelligence in the exercises at the end of this chapter and the section Accessing Broader Mind Through Meditation and Prayer on page 139.

Thought Transmission

If our brains can act as receiving stations, can they also act as transmitting stations? That is, instead of receiving thoughts from the universe, what would happen if we held a dominant thought in mind and sustained it? Could we send this thought out to the universe? Might our thoughts, as waves of quantum information, interact with other waves to create new possibilities—new natural holograms?

To answer these questions, we turn to another quirk of the quantum world called the *observer effect*. The observer effect refers to the ability of conscious intention to affect subatomic behavior. Yes, according to quantum physics, it is possible that our thoughts can affect the universe on its tiniest level; this is not science fiction. It has been supported by nearly a century of experiments in quantum physics, starting with the first experiments conducted by the physicist Niels Bohr in the early part of the twentieth century.

What these experiments have shown is that the simple act of *looking* for a subatomic particle (such as an electron or photon) with the intent to measure that particle can actually cause the particle to appear where it was intended to be found. The particle didn't exist as a single object before it was observed. It existed as only as a multiple-state possibility. It was the *act* of observing or measuring it that converted it to a single object.

You may ask, "How does simply looking for or thinking about a particle make it come into existence?" Good question! Scientists have been debating this for years. One theory refers us back to quantum entanglement; that is, if everything in the universe shares quantum information, then our minds—as combined waves of quantum information—must be transmitting to the universe the desired presence and state of the particle.

As we discussed earlier, matter waves are not defined objects in our spacetime. They are energy spread out across nonlocal space in what is known as a state of *superposition*. A superpositioned state is one in which matter is virtual. In this state, matter has no defined existence and lives only in potential; what makes it real is its interaction with another wave. Recall that when two waves interact, they create a combined pattern, and it is this pattern that holds the information about the particle and defines the particle's state in this spacetime. Thus, when our thought waves interact with a wave of a potential electron or photon, they define the state and location for that particle.

The observer effect so astounded early pioneers of quantum physics that one British astrophysicist and cosmologist, Sir Arthur Eddington, once wrote, "The mind has the power to affect groups of atoms and even tamper with the odds of atomic behavior, and ... even the course of the world is not predetermined by the physical laws but may be altered by the uncaused volition of human beings."

This sentiment was echoed by a fellow cosmologist, Sir James Jean, who added, "Mind no longer appears as an accidental intruder into the realms of matter; we are beginning to suspect that we ought rather to hail it as the creator and governor of the realm of matter."

The observer effect refers to the ability of our thoughts to affect the small-scale world, but how effective can our thoughts be on the large-scale world? After all, the universe is a very big place, and there is quite a bit of "cross talk." Moreover, large-scale objects and events are comprised of many waves and particles—how are our thoughts going to make a ripple in this vast sea of interaction?

Obviously, a random thought here or there is not going to do it. For instance, we're not going to suddenly manifest a shiny new car out of thin air with a simple wish. The universe tends toward an overall stable balance as a result of its multiple source interactions, and this is the reason it adheres to statistical rules of probability.

However, a single dominant thought repeated over and over again is much more likely to make a difference simply because it is being transmitted louder and clearer and continuously into the universe. Broadcasted long enough, its chances of interacting with other waves and creating a new possibility are enhanced.

Therefore, by focusing unwavering on a single outcome, we may hope for tiny, gradual changes over time, especially in those things that are small and already in a state of flux, such as minor events and ongoing mental and physical processes. Within limits, we may set in motion a series of microevents that can lead to a desired outcome and our fervent prayers being answered. For example, we might be able to "nudge" innate self-healing tendencies. After all, if chronic worry can make us sick and depressed, then chronic focusing on a positive outcome should make us happy and well.

That we have some influence on the unfolding of outcomes was believed by theoretical physicist David Bohm. According to Bohm, the future—like fluid waves of a flowing hologram—is not yet crystallized. Though broad trends may become established in the implicate order, smaller individual events (emerging wave patterns) are yet to settle. Bohm's view is expressed as such: "When people dream of accidents correctly and do not take the plane or ship, it is not the actual future that they were seeing. It was merely something in the present which is implicate and moving toward making that future. In fact, the future they saw differed from the actual future because they altered it."

Factors that Enhance Thought Transmission

There are several things we can do to enhance our chances for a desired outcome (see also Factors that Enhance a Solution State in chapter 5):

SPECIFY THE OUTCOME

The first thing we can do to enhance our chances of manifesting a desired outcome is to concentrate solely on those thoughts that are most relevant to the outcome and quiet down all other extraneous thoughts; this increases the strength of the signal we broadcast to the universe. Too many competing thoughts invites mental noise and dilutes our focused intentions. The key is to focus on those thoughts that are central and that will have the most impact on the manifestation of the outcome. For example, if our desire is to heal the body, then we focus on those thoughts most related to the specific area of the body needing healing—not on peripheral thoughts, such as those associated with other body areas or issues like work or relationships.

FOCUS ON FACTORS IN FLUX

Recall Bohm's representation of the future as a fluid hologram. We'll have a better chance of realizing a desired outcome if we focus on those actions and events that are still unfolding rather than on those that have already been crystallized. Before crystallization, events are fluid and therefore open to influence. For example, we'll have a better chance of healing the body by focusing early on in an illness on innate, ongoing repair processes rather than after internal states have become too disorganized.

Focus On a Vivid Outcome

We've all heard the saying, "A picture is worth a thousand words." What this saying means is that a detailed image carries much more information than a single thought or word. In terms of manifesting outcomes, this means that when we visualize a desired outcome in vivid detail, we in fact broadcast much more information to the universe than we would with a simple thought or wish.

For example, if you desire to increase the odds of manifesting healing, don't simply wish for it. Instead, mentally picture the body healing with most of your imaginary senses, such as sight, sound, and hearing. For instance, you might see cells realign, hear the free-flowing movement of circulation, and feel energy recharging the body.

Moreover, when visualizing a vivid outcome, we see it in our mind's eye as if it is happening at the moment. Recall that at the level of the deeper universal mind, there is no "time" as we know it. In the quantum field of possibility, everything is happening all at once and not in a linear time frame. What we envision in our session will be the possibility we trigger. So we don't wish for the outcome to happen in the future, or that is what we will most likely get: an outcome that is always in a state of becoming. By envisioning the outcome as if it is already present, we instead trigger the outcome happening now.

Focus On Closely Entangled Factors

Though the entire universe is interconnected, subsets of it are more closely entangled than other parts of it. For example, each of our bodies arose from the same DNA molecule, so we are more entangled with our bodies than with external people and things. This is supported by research. One such study conducted by William Braud, PhD, is of particular interest. Dr. Braud had subjects sit and meditate on preventing blood cells from breaking down in a test tube and found that subjects were able to sustain the integrity of their own blood cells longer than the cells of others. (See his book *Distant Mental Influence* for details of this research.)

For this reason, if we want to increase our chances of manifesting a desired outcome, we should focus more on our own actions and body processes than on external factors, such as other people and processes. For example, when healing the body, we might spend more time visualizing innate healing processes leading to a desired outcome than on visualizing an external therapy leading to a desired outcome.

Moreover, similar research has shown that those with a strong emotional bond are more likely to influence each other at a distance than strangers or those in the general public. Thus, we're more likely to realize an outcome that involves praying for the healing of or the support of those to whom we feel emotionally connected.

Focus On an Outcome Repeatedly

Recall that repeated focus builds up tiny changes over time. Therefore, for the success of an outcome, we should focus on and visualize it unfolding repeatedly on a regular basis until it does manifest. But remember: we always end each session seeing the outcome happening at the moment.

Monitor Focus

Finally, to realize the success of a desired outcome, we should monitor our thoughts from time to time to be sure we remain focused on our desired outcome. Left to our own devices, our minds are likely to slip back into doubt and negative thinking. Since it takes sustained thought to produce quantum effects, we don't have to police every thought we have—just the thoughts we dwell on. If we should find ourselves dwelling on doubt or negative thoughts, we simply shift back to our desired outcome. The more time we can stay here, the better.

Enhancing Thought Reception and Transmission

As we have seen, our connection with the universal field means we can both receive and exert influence on it while in a calm, prayerful, or meditative state. Both receiving and exerting influence can be helpful in reaching desired outcomes. For one, we may receive insight from the field that will point us to our next step toward our target objective. For example, we may glean insight on the best places or actions to take to obtain a desired job. Or, we may exert influence on the field by concentrating in detail on the outcome and triggering waves of its possibility. For instance, we might receive a call for a job after vividly imagining receiving that call.

However, it is important to mention that receiving and exerting influence are not equal in their ability to obtain desired outcomes. In general, receiving information from the field offers a better chance of obtaining desired outcomes than exerting intentions on it. This is for two main reasons.

First, the universal field holds much more information than our conscious minds and therefore knows much more about what outcomes are best for us and how to obtain them. Too often, the outcomes we desire consciously are selected from the ego.

Second, our conscious intentions tend to be limited due to many influences present in the field that cancel each other out. Recall that the universal field tends toward an overall balance as a result of its many competing sources of information, much like a thermostat attempts to maintain a set point in response to fluctuations in ambient temperature.

For these reasons, it is best to check first with the larger field of information when determining our target and the best course of action for attaining it. After doing so, we may visualize this objective and its associated actions to increase the odds of its manifestation. Together, this two-step process should guide us through a series of events that eventually bring us to our desired outcome. We, in effect, co-create the outcome with the larger field.

As mentioned earlier, though, our job is not done even after our prayer or meditative sessions. We still need to be observant of daily opportunities that may arise as a result of our sessions. Our natural inclination will be to return to our habitual ways. We may get caught up again in familiar concerns, become distracted, dwell on doubt and negativity, and ignore inner wisdom or outer opportunities. By staying observant, we will avoid such pitfalls and keep sight of our desired objective as well as any insight or op-portunities associated with it.

The biggest help will be staying in touch with our broader inner mind. It will guide us along the way. We do this by holding onto faith, staying recep-tive to subtle inner information, and avoiding the urge to forge ahead with only the limited conscious mind. The ego or focal mind will want to main-tain its illusory control and focus narrowly on obvious external data. We need to be aware of this tendency so we do not get cut off from our larger awareness, lose our intuitive bearings, and allow fear and doubt of what is out of sight to overcome us. In doing so, we will be in a better position to attain our desired outcome.

Accessing Broader Mind Through Meditation and Prayer

The notion that there is connection to a larger intelligence within is not new. For thousands of years, mystics, sages, and ordinary folk alike have talked about connecting with an inner intelligence in two of the most common forms of calm focus: meditation and prayer.

Many accounts speak of thoughtful seekers retreating to simple envi-ronments such as caves, deserts, and forests to engage in quiet communi-cation with this larger intelligence: "Jesus often withdrew to lonely places and prayed."(Luke 5:16, NIV)

EASTERN MEDITATION

In Eastern meditation, according to the ancient Hindu philosophy of Vedanta, one attains communion with a larger intelligence by quieting everyday thoughts (which sully the mind) and observing deeper areas of mind. The process is likened to a settling stream. Just as the bottom of a stream can be clearly seen when mud settles, deeper areas of mind are revealed when one settles surface thoughts.

In this deep state of "pure awareness," one gets past the illusion of the physical self (called the illusion of Maya) and "awakens" to the realization that everything in the universe is a manifestation of one consciousness, called Brahman. More importantly, one realizes that each individual consciousness, Atman, is but a small distillation of this source consciousness.

At the point of this realization, one is said to be "one with Brahman" or "one with all of existence" and have the awareness of the universe itself; and, according to the ancient Hindu sage Patanjali, develops a "purity" and "luminosity" of thought and an ability to see the "true nature" of things.

This realization that we are one with universal consciousness is encapsulated in the verse of the Katha Upanishad (a sacred Hindu text): "Tat tvam Asi" or "You are that," meaning "You are Brahman." In the later writings of the eighth-century philosopher and teacher Adi Shankara, primarily in his work *The Crest-Jewel of Discrimination*, he writes, "As being essentially pure consciousness, the oneness between the Real and the Self is known by the awakened."

WESTERN PRAYER

In Western prayer, particularly according to the Gnostic gospels, one finds the truth of God by quieting the mind and going within. This is alluded to in the Coptic Gospel of Thomas, verse 49: "Jesus said, 'Blessed are the solitary and elect, for you will find the Kingdom. For you are from it, and to it you will return.'"

Other more well-known, biblical verses that allude to finding God through quiet perception include Luke 17:20–21, NIV: "The kingdom of God is not something that can be observed, nor will people say, 'Here it is,' or 'There it is,' because the kingdom of God is in your midst," and Psalm 46:10, NIV: "Be still, and know that I am God." Likewise, in 1 Kings 19:11 of the Old Testament, Elijah, one of the early prophets of Judaism, found God's words not forcefully in a strong wind, earthquake, or fire, but in a still, small voice—a voice that could only be heard in a quiet state of mind.

The need for a quiet, thoughtful mind when addressing God is also implied in Matthew 6:6, NIV. Here, Jesus urged his followers to pray mindfully in seclusion: "But when you pray, go into your room, close the door and pray to your Father, who is unseen. Then your Father, who sees what is done in secret, will reward you."

Broadening Awareness in Meditation

In meditation, broadening awareness is called *mindfulness meditation*, which—just as we saw in the calm open focus exercises in this book—involves attending to all stimuli in one's awareness at once. Mindfulness meditation teaches one to become detached in one's observations; this detachment not only leads to an opening of thoughts previously blocked by narrower focus, it also leads to greater insight.

One of the greatest benefits of meditating is that it teaches us to simply sit and observe our thoughts and emotions without getting caught up in them. A person may, for example, observe his or her thoughts as clouds floating by. In doing so, one may be able to be more objective about oneself and how he or she reacts in certain circumstances, thereby allowing the person to begin to change his or her problematic reactions. Since this type of meditation leads to personal insight, it is often called *insight meditation*.

Broadening Awareness in Prayer

In prayer, broadening awareness is called *contemplative prayer*. This type of prayer is an undirected form of prayer. When one prays contemplatively, one does not seek a specific outcome from God but is instead receptive to what God has to say.

To do this type of prayer, one simply poses a question to God and then waits openly for an answer. Questions are typically aimed at understanding a problem and one's options with it. E.g., "God, what is needed most in this situation?"

For a contemplative prayer to be effective, one has to put away preconceived notions of what he or she thinks the answer should be and have faith in God's answer. This answer may come in a variety of subtle forms, as we saw earlier in the open questions section, and one has to be patient in receiving it. Again, receiving requires an open, receptive mode.

CONCENTRATING AWARENESS IN MEDITATION

In meditation, concentrating awareness is called *single-point meditation*. This type of meditation involves immersing in the details of a single target, such as a candle flame, the breath, or a word, phrase, or image. As a result of this immersion, one "becomes one with the target."

As we saw earlier, immersing into body imagery can have profound self-regulatory effects. The Buddhist monks in Tibet discussed in chapter 5 are a perfect example. Simply by meditating in detail on heat imagery, these amazing monks were able to survive deadly freezing temperatures.

CONCENTRATING AWARENESS IN PRAYER

In prayer, concentrating awareness is associated with the *petition* or *asking prayer*. Unlike contemplative prayer, this type of prayer is directive. One is not openly receptive to God's input at this time, rather he or she is focused on petitioning God for the manifestation of one outcome. E.g., "God, help me to stand strong in the face of this difficulty."

In petitioning God, one might visualize oneself engaged in a specific outcome and ask God to co-create it; this way, one is very clear about what they are asking for. Concentrating awareness in prayer requires sustained focus, which is another way of saying faith. Sustained focus or faith leads to desired outcomes as supported by several verses in the New Testament:

- But when you ask, you must believe and not doubt, because the one who doubts is like a wave of the sea, blown and tossed by the wind. (James 1:6, NIV)

- Truly I tell you, if anyone says to this mountain, "Go, throw yourself into the sea," and does not doubt in their heart but

believes that what they say will happen, it will be done for
them. Therefore I tell you, whatever you ask for in prayer,
believe that you have received it, and it will be yours.
(Mark 11:23–24, NIV)

- Ask and it will be given to you; seek and you will find; knock
and the door will be opened to you. For everyone who asks
receives; the one who seeks finds; and to the one who knocks,
the door will be opened. (Matthew 7:7–8, NIV)

Collectively, what these passages tell us is that the key to a successful outcome is a single-minded and sustained focus on that outcome in the absence
of doubt. If we seek but deep down doubt, we're focused on doubt and not
the outcome we want. By removing all doubt and focusing repeatedly on an
imagined or prayed-for outcome, we are more likely to realize this outcome.

Thought Research

So is there any direct experimental evidence for our ability to remotely receive
information or influence outcomes as we do in prayer or meditation? The answer is yes. Since the discovery of quantum physics nearly a century ago, there
have been hundreds of studies conducted at major universities and labs around
the world supporting the notion that a calmly focused mind can both remotely
receive and transmit information in small but statistically significant ways.

While sitting in controlled settings, subjects have been able to receive information about distant people and places they have never visited as well as
influence living and nonliving things both simple and complex—including
random number generators, water molecules, microbes, cells, organ tissues,
body processes, and even mental and emotional states.

Apparently, the more influential subjects have been able to receive or
transmit information statistically more often than chance by tuning into the
target and "becoming one" with it; this has appeared to occur regardless of

time and distance, presumably as a result of the nonlocal quantum entangle-ment between the receiver/sender and the target. For more information, check out the section of Research in Distant Mental Effects at the end of this book.

Harvesting Broader Mind Exercises

In the following three exercises, we will learn how to access this broader mind using a calm inner focus. We start by first getting acquainted with it, and then we learn to receive and transmit information with it. In doing so, we hope to stimulate greater insight and influence over problem situations.

Exercise 10.1: Tuning In to the Broader Mind

Contact with this larger intelligence brings not only wisdom but also a feeling of great comfort and connectedness. Though we may at times feel alone and separate in our everyday, limited conscious mind, a deep connection with this universal mind shows us that we are never alone. It is as if we always have an unseen partner who's there to help. In times of confusion and chaos, we can go to this deeper intelligence for safe haven and guidance. Here, fear subsides, the body heals, and we find "the peace of God that surpasses all understanding."

The connection is there inside us, since this larger intelligence pervades all things, including our minds and bodies. We can sense it more directly when we relax and free our minds of thought. By doing so, we begin to dissolve the boundary between the larger intelligence and our minds and bodies. We become open to its boundless, formless state.

In this exercise, we're going to learn how to relax and sit quietly and immerse ourselves in this deeper intelligence.

1. To begin, enter into calm focus and simply observe the rhythm of your breathing. Do not alter it or get caught up in your thinking. Just focus completely on how your chest rises and falls with each breath. Imagine your breathing as waves rolling

gently on and off a shore. Follow the rhythm of these waves. Immerse yourself in them. Focus on this and nothing else.

2. As you immerse yourself in these waves, imagine you are simply a mind without a body, floating in these waves of rhythm. Stay in the heart of this rhythm and imagine you are making contact with all of nature around you. Sense the intelligence of this nature. Imagine the presence of this intelligence as a peaceful calm enveloping you. Feel the unconditional love it has for you. Feel it embrace you. Sit quietly and immerse yourself in this calm, loving presence. When you are done, thank the peaceful presence for being there and return your focus to the room.

This exercise is a favorite of many of my clients. It not only provides a welcome break when things become a little too hectic, but it also renews the spirit.

If the experience seems vague or subtle at first, keep practicing. As you learn to quiet your thoughts and let go, you will begin to experience it more and more. Eventually, as your eyes become open, you will notice this intelligence everywhere around you: in the beauty of nature, in the harmony of your life, in the goodness of others, and in you, flowing through and inspiring your very thoughts and actions. Recall the words of Jesus: "Behold, the kingdom of God is in the midst of you."

Exercise 10.2: Dialoguing with the Broader Mind

In the following exercise, we will be imagining a dialogue with a representative of this larger intelligence. This conversation should enhance our ability to get spontaneous responses from it. For instance, we may use an image of a wise sage to represent our subconscious connection to this larger intelligence. Imaginary dialogue is an excellent way to enhance the insight we get from our broader inner mind. Mental pictures are concrete and provide a tangible dimension to our inner voice when coupled with open questions.

1. Close your eyes and enter into calm focus. Imagine you are standing in front of a large door or gateway. Enter through the door and notice that you are in a beautiful garden court-yard. All around you are a variety of colorful flowers and trees, fountains, and stone architecture. Feel yourself in the midst of this experience as you absorb the rich sights of lush vegetation, the soothing sounds of running water, the feel of cool air, and the smell of gentle fragrance.

2. In front of you is a stone pathway leading to a circular en-closure at the center of the courtyard. There you notice benches surrounding a fire. Slowly walk down the path and sit on the closest bench in front of the fire. Feel the fire's warmth as it illuminates the area bathing the courtyard in a soft glow.

3. Imagine now a shimmering light behind the bench opposite you. This light slowly takes human form and becomes the image of a wise sage. Notice this person's dress and attributes. You sense the love and compassion coming from this person and that this person is here to help and knows you better than anyone else.

4. Invite the wise sage to sit down in front of you and ask the sage the following open questions about an issue troubling you: "What is the real issue here? What is really bothering me? What is causing most of the problem? What is needed most to remedy this situation? How do I begin to do this?" Wait for a response and trust that it will come. Let whatever comes to mind be there and ask for further clarification. Continue dialoguing with this inner sage, asking further Solution

Targeting questions as you allow the process to flow freely, bouncing ideas back and forth, without censoring anything.

5. When you've come to some insight or direction on the issue, thank the wise sage for his or her help. When you are ready, open your eyes and return your focus to the room. Be prepared to test these actions in your situation.

If you have trouble receiving insight from open dialogue, imagine you are looking at the open flame in front of you (or, if you'd like, a still pond) and ask your inner mind to place a word, phrase, or image in this flame that best represents this insight. Then ask further, "What is this connected to in my life?" Or, simply go about your normal routine and wait for the answer. Seize upon any opportunity that arises.

For best results, practice this exercise at least once a day for ten to twenty minutes to build your inner communication.

Teaching clients how to contact inner wisdom is a regular feature in my private practice. Paula had been suffering from unresolved fatigue and sadness for some time. When she entered into calm focus and met with her inner wise sage, she was surprised when it told her that the fatigue and sadness had come from losing sight of her passion in life—organizing events—which she hadn't done in years. She was advised to go out and begin doing so. When she did, she noticed the fatigue and sadness start to lift. However, soon after, she stopped doing events and began to feel the fatigue and sadness slip back. She returned to her inner sanctuary and met with her wise sage again, who then told her that she feared failing but she should simply follow her heart. If she did so, her true nature would unfold instinctually and she would find success. Paula then followed the sage's advice and returned to event planning and now continues to have a zest for life, free of fatigue and sadness.

Like Paula, you too may derive similar insights from your inner intelligence that may be helpful in troubling situations. Give the exercise a try and see what you find.

Exercise 10.3: Utilizing Inner Insights to Produce a Solution State

In this exercise, we're going to take the insight gained from dialoguing with an imaginary representative of our universal mind and immerse ourselves in the details of this solution in order to evoke the manifestation of this solution.

1. Enter into calm focus again and build a sensory picture of the answer given to you by your inner mind during the dialogue process you completed in exercise 10.2. If your inner intelligence told you to take action on an issue or told you that a certain state of mind is needed to remedy a situation, imagine seeing yourself engaging in these conditions, hear the words spoken by you and others, and—most importantly—feel in your body what it is like to have these conditions.

2. Repeat this scenario three or four times for about ten minutes. At the end of ten minutes, turn the image over to your inner mind to carry out. Think of it as a request that you are sending it. You may, for example, say, "I give this to you to fulfill. I ask you to please co-create this with me. Thank you for helping me with this change."

3. At this point, let go and trust that your inner intelligence knows more than your conscious mind about how to manifest this desire. Letting go shows that you have a firm faith in the outcome and are devoid of doubt. Recall, though, that we don't stay idle. You are co-creating with your inner intelligence, so you need to do your conscious part. Go out now and stay open

to opportunities in which you utilize these newly acquired conditions and act as if they are already a part of you. Your inner wisdom will do the rest.

ELEVEN

Observing from Broader Mind

An ostrich with its head in the sand is just as
blind to opportunity as to disaster.
—Unknown

As we have seen throughout this book, getting past life's difficulties and reaching desired goals requires a degree of oversight. We have to get our "heads out of the sand" once in a while to see where we're going and if we've made it. When we don't, we often get derailed.

Still, maintaining overall focus is not always easy. Both life challenges and old habits will test our ability to stay observant. Obstacles may come along to fixate us, or we may simply slip into autopilot and stop monitoring our progress. The result is that we often fall into the trap of a limited focus and lose sight of our target destination and to what end our thoughts and actions are headed.

Because unintentional detouring is such an insidious occurrence in the change process, this chapter is aimed at helping you increase awareness of it—especially when it first arises—so you can get back on track and reach desired objectives.

Oversight is maintained when we keep watch on our focus. Recall that an unattended focus is a focus on subconscious autopilot; and a focus on autopilot will move to what's familiar, which are the same thoughts and actions that have been entrenched with use.

Sometimes auto reactions are useful, such as in emergency situations when we don't have time to think through a conscious decision—e.g., jumping out of the way of a speeding car. But many times these reactions are rigid and unproductive. For example, if we have been telling ourselves since childhood that we are not good enough, then our first reaction when criticized is likely to feel inadequate.

The key is to know when to engage auto reactions and when not to. If we cannot disengage them, we are likely to be compelled to think and act in fixed ways. Disengaging auto reactions requires that we know when we are in them, which is also not always easy! For example, we may be so caught up with the view that we are inadequate that we are unaware we're quickly defending this illusory perception or that we have other qualities that can disprove it.

We tend to not know we are in a fixed view for several reasons. For one, recall that when you're trapped in one view, you do not have access to other views; so the one view starts to look like your only reality. Two, the longer you're in one view, the more accustomed you become to it, so you don't realize it is influencing everything you see and do. Third, you often don't know you are in a fixed view because of how quickly such a view pops into being in a triggering situation; you don't realize you are limited to feelings of inadequacy when they appear instantly upon hearing any criticism. A equals B so quickly that you don't stop to wonder if A *should* equal B.

Undetected fixed views will run our lives and keep us stuck, repeating the same things and suffering the same consequences over and over again. The longer and more frequently we dwell on them, the greater their illusion, the greater our emotional reaction to them, and the harder it is to escape from them.

Identifying a Fixed View

Fortunately, there is something we can do to become more aware of when we have derailed into a fixed view, and that is to observe the body. Recall that we discussed that we can assess our current state by observing the body. The body often provides reliable clues of a fixed focus even though we may not be conscious of it; this is because—as we also discussed in chapter 5—the body will tend to respond to what is in mind, and will do so whether the mental activity is conscious or not.

Therefore, by observing body signs in the form of emotions, tension, or sensations, we can get an idea of when we are under the spell of a fixed, limited view. Once aware, we then can bring its hidden contents into focal awareness and get a read on them. For example, by observing tension in our body, we may discover that we are fixating on angry thoughts. To direct our attention to the body, we may ask ourselves, "What is going on inside me at this moment?"

The first thing we look for is low-level tension, which is typically found in the areas we normally accumulate stress, such as the jaw, neck, shoulders, and back. The gut or stomach area is particularly sensitive to our thoughts, so look for any tension there as well. These areas are our *habitual reaction points*. Next, we look to our breathing, since breathing is another body reaction that is sensitive to our mental focus. Is the breathing high in the chest, shallow and rapid? Or is it lower in the belly, deeper and more rhythmic? High, rapid breathing is a sign we are reacting negatively to thoughts in our head.

Finally, we look for any negative feelings. The feeling we are experiencing at the moment may be pronounced or it may be subtle, a feeling in the background. It can range from vague tension, irritation, or unease to acute anger, fear, or sadness. We pay special attention to any feelings that have been there for a while or that return again and again, since these feelings tend to indicate the presence of habitual thoughts.

We call these body signs *detection markers*. It is a good idea to monitor these markers on a regular basis, especially when challenges arise; this only takes a moment or so.

Auto fixation can happen fast, especially when we are presented with a challenge. During these times, it is a good idea to catch the autofocus tendency before it has a chance to take over. This may mean becoming alert to detection markers as soon as the challenge presents itself. Any delay may allow conditioned programming to get the upper hand. The moment we react mindlessly, the autopilot is in charge.

Signs that auto fixation is kicking in include sudden changes in body sensation or mood (such as rapid breathing or tensing), a flash of irritation or fear, or an urge to respond. The moment you detect any of these markers, let that be a reminder to step out and observe.

Zooming Out of a Fixed View

As we have learned so far, observing our reactions from a distance puts us in a more objective position to explore them and see what is generating them. The moment we become aware of our automatic reactions, we are no longer trapped in them. We begin to see their impact on us, how much we are caught up in them, and why we engage in them. Put simply, we get a glimpse into the nature of our subconscious programming.

The key is to sit calmly and patiently and observe the reaction to see what thoughts might be behind it. Start first with what you are feeling. Are you experiencing any unease or discomfort? Or is it a full-blown feeling like fear, anger, or sadness? Is the feeling nagging you all the time? Or is it only at certain times? If so, what times?

Next, explore the thoughts behind the feeling. What could you be saying to yourself that is making you feel this way? Is there a critical voice there in your head, judging? If so, what is it saying?

As you bring these thoughts into focal awareness, you may find that your reaction to them becomes amplified. Your desire at this moment may be to resist, run from, or get caught up in these thoughts. Avoid doing this, otherwise you leave these conditioned thoughts in place.

Instead, remind yourself that you are not your thoughts. These thoughts may be arising within your awareness, but you are separate and more than these thoughts. In fact, you keep in mind that much of these thoughts are products of subconscious programming, outputs of brain machinery. They are in the foreground. You are the witness or awareness in the background, observing these conditioned thoughts.

To get a feel for this separation, observe your thoughts right now. As you observe them, notice also that there is an observer watching them. Here is "you," and there are the thoughts you are observing. You are the observing awareness, and that awareness is separate from thought. To make this distinction more clear, say to yourself as you observe your thoughts, "I am here, and there are those thoughts over there." The moment you make this distinction, you identify your true self and realize you are the larger awareness beyond thought.

Likewise, we may distance ourselves from thoughts by remembering to identify the central factor and frame it with a word or phrase; this will create a bit of a gap between us and the thoughts. For example, if we find that we are dwelling on all the hurt we've experienced from previous relationships, we can step back and say, "There is that overall theme again of identifying myself too strongly with my relationships."

Once we've identified the central factor, we redirect ourselves back to where we want to be: our target objective. Recall that we do this by putting our current state to the target test. We may ask ourselves at this moment, "Are these thoughts I am experiencing right now helping or hindering me from getting where I want to go?" If the answer is that they are hindering us, then we have to let them go and focus on more constructive thoughts.

This is where we have to be real with ourselves. It does not matter whether you believe these thoughts or not; what matters is that you want to move forward and not continue to add extra suffering to your life. You have to ask the next questions: "What are other ways I can look at this situation? What other thoughts would be more helpful in getting me closer to where I want to be? What thoughts would be most helpful?"

Often, when we recognize that our fixed way of thinking is not helping us but adding to our suffering, we can let these thoughts go and start focusing in a different direction. You know you've let go of a fixed view and are on to a more constructive path when you feel options opening up and a growing sense of peace.

When we regain our overall bearings and our direction is clearer, we then can respond more mindfully and flexibly. Though we may still be compelled to think and react in the old way, we aren't reacting mindlessly. We are aware of what is causing the reaction and can make a conscious choice to stay the course. The fixed programming then loses much of its power over us.

To ensure you step out at critical reaction times, it is a good idea to mentally rehearse anticipated problems ahead of time. With time and practice, you should see more success at staying on track and reaching desired objectives.

Kate was born with one leg somewhat longer than the other. As she went through childhood, she was teased repeatedly for this attribute. Though she suffered as a child, she felt that she had overcome these experiences as an adult. She went on to win marathons, become a physiotherapist, and drive herself to high levels of achievement, becoming the best in her class. One day she found herself in deep depression and questioning the meaning of her life. "What am I doing and what is it all for?" she wondered.

Kate came to me and we began working on learning how to enter calm focus. After weeks of training and practice with separating herself from her thinking, she discovered that she harbored a great deal of anger about her condition and that deep down, she did not feel good enough and needed to prove to the world that she was. This fixed notion had been carried for so long that Kate was unaware it was driving much of her thoughts and actions. As a result, every time something bad happened to her, she would dwell on the notion over and over again.

With this insight, we then began practicing Exercise 5.3: Evoking a Solution State for several weeks. Slowly, Kate started noticing the anger subside and the depression lift. She no longer believed this negative notion to be the truth of her. Though some of the hurt is still there, she understands it better, and it does not have the same effect on her as before. She said, "I just don't waste my time on it anymore."

We now work on exploring her desired target state and how her life will be different with this newfound knowledge. Kate says today that her life is much lighter and freer, and she does things now not to prove anything but because she enjoys them.

For further practice at separating from fixed thoughts, try the exercises at the end of this chapter. With repeated practice, you may find it easier to get out of fixed thinking. Likewise, to understand the separation between the observing mind and the robot-like brain that generates conditioned thoughts, see the following section.

Mind Versus Brain

Detaching from the brain and its automatic generation of thought is not as difficult as one might imagine. Some believe that the brain and mind are one; this is the conventional view. But others believe that the two are separate and that they interact with and influence each other. In this view, the brain is a machine—a neural receiver and transmitter—and the mind is an integrated energy and information construct. The two interact via fields permeating the brain. In this way, changes in brain function can effect changes in consciousness, and vice versa.

The notion that brain and mind are separate but interrelated starts with the observation that no evidence exists to show that mind or consciousness—or memories, for that matter—are located in any specific place in the brain. Nowhere can we say that certain thoughts or conscious experiences are produced by the same brain areas. For instance, you will not always get the image of your aunt Mildred every time you stimulate the same cortical spot in your brain.

In fact, it appears that mind or consciousness is associated with several (sometimes remote) areas of the brain working together. That is, during a reported conscious experience, several brain areas are active (as displayed on imaging devices), showing a correlation between brain activity and electromagnetic fields. This has led some researchers to conclude that consciousness is a field phenomenon—either associated with the electromagnetic fields permeating the brain or deeper quantum field processes, or both.

More specifically, mind or consciousness is associated with the information stored in these fields. Fields, like all things in nature, are comprised of waves; and as we saw in chapter 10, waves link information. Accordingly, it may be that the mind is associated with the integrated information in these fields. Information integrates in fields when waves *resonate* with the same frequency. When waves resonate, they "tune in" to each other, so to speak, much like tuning forks. When this occurs, they then share information. We saw this in chapter 10; that is, when two waves interact, they create a third, more complex wave that contains information about the first and second waves. Think of how we get a station on the radio—we dial our receiver so that it tunes in to the same frequency being broadcasted by the station.

In the case of the brain, since several areas are active, there exist electromagnetic fields accompanying this activity. When these fields are resonating at the same frequency, they act as one coherent field to integrate their information. This integration is accompanied by a unified conscious experience: "I am sitting here, looking at this orange and purple sunset, smelling the pine, feeling the gentle breeze, and feeling a sense of peace."

As integrated information, mind may be stored in electromagnetic and quantum fields. After all, all fields have their roots in the quantum field. At the quantum level, this integrated information that is mind would then be entangled with all other information stored in the universe. In short, our individual minds could be entangled with the one universal mind!

Because of its dual entanglement, the mind could quite possibly communicate with both the brain and the universe at large. This connection would likely be mediated by field effects. In the case of the brain, the field of consciousness would communicate with the brain via electromagnetic and/or quantum field processes; in the case of the universe, through the quantum field.

Awareness would then fluctuate, depending on the degree of communication the mind has with the brain. When the mind resonates fully with the input coming from the brain (the brain's sensory and automatic processes), the mind operates within a narrow range of awareness. It receives only local information and gets fused with the brain's illusion.

In contrast, when the mind ignores the thought machine and focuses calmly in the stillness, it increases its awareness of its universal connection. At this stage, the mind gains access to nonlocal information and more original thoughts. Here, mind acts as a universal field phenomenon.

The *false self* is the mind identified with the brain and what the local senses bring it. The *true self* is the mind aware of its larger, nonlocal connection. The false self is in the foreground; it is usually the one we identify with the most because the input supporting it is often the loudest, clearest, and most concrete. On the other hand, the true self lies in the background; it is pure awareness that is connected to the enduring information of the universe. Typically it is seldom accessed because the input that supports it is subtle and vague. But when we observe from this larger awareness, we are always most wise, at peace, and in the flow.

In his book *Doors of Perception*, the novelist and philosopher Aldous Huxley put it aptly: "The brain does not produce mind, it reduces mind … each of us is potentially 'Mind at Large.' But in so far as we are animals, our business at all cost is to survive. To make biological survival possible, Mind at Large has to be funneled through the reducing valve of the brain and nervous system. What comes out the other end is a measly trickle of the kind of consciousness which will help us stay alive on the surface of this particular planet."

Huxley saw consciousness as a fundamental property of the universe that produced individual consciousness when filtered through the brain. We can choose which side of the funnel we want to operate on. Sometimes, we need to pay attention to the external world, as when we are driving. At other times, we need to pay attention to things outside the brain (and its concrete senses), especially when we require a look at our larger life. In this case, we need to shift from a narrow, external focus to a broader, internal one where we can tune in to our nonlocal connection and gather intuitive wisdom.

Likewise, when we need to step out of our conditioned thoughts, a good analogy to keep in mind is to view our thoughts as computer software and our observing presence as the keyboard operator. Who is running the show? Is it the software program or is it the operator? If we allow our conditioned thoughts to kick in all the time without our conscious input, it's like having a computer program run without the operator. Nothing new happens. Therefore, in order to adapt to changing conditions, we need to stay in command as the observing operator and update the program accordingly; otherwise, we are not the ones in charge, the program is.

Like a computer, the brain is good at processing information and outputting it in the form of actions. But the best actions come when we, the observing presence (the operator), integrate the information gathered by the brain and direct the show. When we are directing the show, the brain is a useful tool. The brain's power becomes a problem when we are asleep at the wheel and let it run the show.

Exercise 11.1: Broadening Inner Space

This is a simple exercise for beginning to train your mind to see its separation from thoughts and to see it as a larger awareness in which thinking is only a subset. That is, thinking is only one aspect of our total awareness.

1. Start by relaxing into calm focus and then observe your thinking. As you observe, you may notice an inner dialogue. At certain moments, this dialogue quiets down or pauses. Notice the silence at these times. Be aware of the mental space that holds this silence.

2. Then notice where in the mental space the thoughts emerge. Be aware now of you as the awareness observing both the mental space and the thoughts within this space. Observe the thoughts in the foreground while you acknowledge yourself as the awareness in the background.

As you practice this exercise, you will gradually learn to separate yourself from your thoughts and be able to observe them when you need to at critical times.

Exercise 11.2: Identifying and Defusing Auto Reactions

In this exercise, we are going to practice stepping into the observer mode as soon as we notice a negative state. We will observe the auto thoughts generating this state and begin learning to separate ourselves from them.

1. Think about a situation troubling you lately. Pick a situation that you suspect might reoccur in the future; this way you can plan for the possible event. Regardless, pick a situation that is not too difficult so that you may practice the steps involved without getting overwhelmed. In an earlier example, we used paying the bills.

2. Start the sequence of events as you did in Exercise 5.3: Evoking a Solution State. Observe these events unfold. As you observe, also attend to your emotional and physical reactions.

3. As soon as you become aware of any reactions, tell yourself, "Stop!" Imagine a big red stop sign in your mind's eye. Take one or two deep breaths and slow down and really pay attention to these reactions. Ask yourself, "Am I aware of standing back and observing right now? Or am caught up in my thoughts, losing myself in this situation?" Notice how this questioning begins to separate you from the situation.

4. From this detached perspective, describe the tension or emotion to yourself. How would you label it? Where did you begin to feel it first? Look beneath the reaction to the thoughts accompanying the reaction. There is always internal commentary and interpretations being made. Observe fully. Sometimes these thoughts move quickly, and we may have trouble pinpointing them. Pay special attention to thoughts that recur or seem familiar—like they've been there before. These are conditioned thoughts—the brain's auto-programming. Don't get caught up in these thoughts. Stay above them and simply observe.

5. As you pay attention to these thoughts, see which ones might be triggering the reaction. Identify the link between the thoughts and the reaction. You might, for example, observe anxiety and see what you're saying to yourself as you experience this anxiety. Ask yourself, "What am I thinking or focusing on right now? Could I be looking at this situation in a limited way and creating suffering for myself? Are my thoughts trying to understand the situation

or are they really adding to my discontent? What are these thoughts saying that is causing me to feel anxious?"

6. Next, challenge these thoughts. Recognize them for what they are: products of brain machinery and prior conditioning. Realize also that they are not the only reality. There is always a bigger picture (and other views), and we often do not have these views at first (or ever). Ask yourself at this point, "Is this the only view? What could be other ways to see this situation?" Alternately, "What is most needed in this situation? What can I do to provide this need?" Explore these more constructive thoughts and see what actions you might take in the situation to make things better.

7. After exploring actions, zoom in and enter the scene as an active participant. Rerun the scenario using these newly-identified actions. In the example case of criticism, instead of lashing out, remain calm and talk yourself down. You might say, "This is this person's opinion. I can choose to find something constructive in it or brush it off. But no matter what is said, I can remain calm and in control." As you say this, take a deep breath and release any tension.

8. Finally, rerun the scene again and rehearse the positive scenario several times to reinforce it subconsciously. Do this with all troubling situations that you can anticipate. Remember: in order to change a negative situation, we have to change the thoughts (or view) associated with that situation.

TWELVE

Tying It All Together

Only that day dawns to which we are awake.
—Henry David Thoreau

We started this book with the premise that a calm focus is the best tool for solving problems. Since then we have explored the relationship between our focus and our perceptions of problems and how a calm focus has several advantages to increase our awareness of problems and their solutions.

First and foremost, as a balance of alertness and relaxation, calm focus offers flexible focus control. Within the optimal zone of calm focus, we can rein in thought without fixating on any one thought and as a result, maneuver our focus to see multiple views. One of these views—and the second advantage of calm focus—is a broadening awareness. With a flexible focus, we may maneuver into a detached observer mode and gain greater awareness of a problem. From this vantage point, we may see what can be beyond the problem and move into the third advantage of calm focus—concentrating awareness. In this immersed mode, we absorb ourselves in the details of this solution state and evoke it. Together, these advantages of calm focus provide an efficient way to move from a problem state to a desired solution state.

The benefits don't end there, though. As we saw in chapter 10, a calm inner focus (as experienced in meditation and prayer) can lead to profound awareness and influence over problems, well beyond what we see in a normal state of mind.

Practice, Practice, Practice

Whether we attain the benefits described here depends in large part on our focusing skill. Fortunately, our focus, like any skill, can improve with practice.

The exercises in this book can help. By doing them on a regular basis, you may expect to see your focusing skill improve and the range and power of your problem-solving ability increase. If some of the exercises seem awkward or results are not readily forthcoming, don't get discouraged. Just keep practicing; soon you'll see the exercises get easier and your results improving.

For best results, practice the exercises daily. Establish a routine and try not to miss a session. Start by setting aside at least five minutes a day. Shorter sessions are easier to start and maintain. Build up to ten- or twenty-minute sessions two or three times each day. Remember to do the sessions in a quiet, comfortable place and at a time when you are not tired—otherwise you might fall asleep!

Start by making a list of current problems. From this list, select one that you'd like to solve presently. As we discussed, not every problem is equal. Choosing one ensures that you're focused on the most important problem. Next, go through several cycles of Solution Targeting. Define the problem's central factor, pinpoint and test target actions, and update and refine these actions until you're satisfied with a solution.

Outside of practice sessions, remember to monitor your focus throughout the day. You may use the target chart on page 119 to keep track of progress, but don't worry about a formal setting at these times. When a question or difficulty arises, simply take a moment to stop, silence your thoughts, and submit it to your inner mind; then heed its advice. As you become proficient at calm focusing, you will be able to do it anywhere and anytime, including during busy times and while in traffic or a line.

If you do these things—start small and practice a few minutes a day—in time you will see benefits. Some of these benefits may emerge in as little as three weeks of regular practice. The first thing you'll notice is a state of calm that becomes more and more noticeable each day. As you continue practicing, you will notice insights occurring more often and auto reactions occurring less frequently. Other things you'll begin to notice are

- increased ability to quiet thoughts and sustain clearer focus;

- greater awareness and control over thoughts and feelings;

- improved flexibility to see situations differently and discover insight;

- increased ability to tune in to inner mind for answers;

- heightened physical and mental healing; and

- greater peace and joy.

Defining a Life Goal

Ultimately, what we can expect from regular use of calm focus is a fully conscious and awakened life. Being fully conscious not only allows us to look at ourselves and our habitual reactions more clearly, but it enables us to take stock of our lives and where they are heading. We are free to choose the life we want instead of continuing to tolerate the one we have.

What taking stock does most is simplify our life. Too often in these modern times, we move from day to day without much oversight. Juggling the demands of the day, we seldom have enough time to really think about what we're doing and if it is really fulfilling us. As a result, we engage in mindless busywork or meaningless activities that bring more chaos than order to our lives.

With conscious oversight, however, we can define an overall vision or goal for our lives. With this goal in mind, much of our actions are geared toward a common cause and not scattered about haphazardly. Like a beacon in the distance, the goal can act as a reference point by which we guide our thoughts and actions and navigate life. Important decisions and priorities can be made based on our life goal(s).

Yet, we are also mindful of maintaining an overall balance. We may use the goal to orient our lives, but we are careful not to use it to overly constrain our lives. That is, we set our actions on a goal, but we aren't so fixated on it that we can't be flexible in our approach to it. Rigid fixation on the future (or the past, for that matter) robs us of the present, which is the only real thing we have in any one moment.

Therefore, what we seek to do is just check in once in a while to see if our current path is leading us to where we want to be and, if need be, make a few course corrections; this may mean assessing any current obstacles or avenues, as well as our actions, and determining the best course. Recall that we determine the best course by putting our current actions to the target test ("Is what I am doing now getting me closer to my goal? If not, what actions would get me closer?).

To reach her goals, Nancy thought that she had to put her nose to the grindstone. She felt that if she didn't, her desires would slip away from her. When she encountered obstacles, she would often stress about meeting objectives on time. She strived so hard that she sometimes forgot to stay in a calm focus and approached activities in a hard narrow focus. Not surprisingly, life became drudgery. After practicing calm focus for some time, Nancy now reports greater flexibility with tasks and objectives and can actually enjoy daily activities as well as her accomplishments. I asked her about the cause for this change, and she told me it was her increased ability to monitor her state and relax with situations instead of worrying about all the details or whether she would reach her target "on time." She described this new way of being as freeing. Now when obstacles arise, Nancy remains calm and is confident that no matter what happens, she can keep remaining calm. As a result, she is happier with her life.

How do you determine a worthy goal for your life? Do you look for what can make you happy? Fulfilled? At peace? How do you ask the important questions: "What is the purpose of my life? What am I really trying to accomplish with my life?" At first glance, you'd probably agree that a worthy life goal is one that gives our lives purpose and meaning, a way of saying we matter. But where do we find this purpose and meaning?

Some of us look for it outside ourselves. We seek it in such external things as work, social roles, and material possessions. Often we find these things are not enough; after we get them, we find that we still feel like something is missing, that we are incomplete. What then can fulfill or complete us? We will discover the answer only when we look inside ourselves. It is within that we find our true nature and our place in the larger scheme of things.

It is true that on the surface our lives may appear fragmented and without order or reason; one day we're up, and the next we're down. It's understandable how we may come to think that there is no purpose to it all. But as we discussed earlier, underneath it all there is always a deeper order, and we are part of this order. Therefore, our lives have more meaning and purpose than we realize. A worthy life goal then is to discover how we may uniquely contribute to this order. We do this by bringing the important questions to our deeper, broader mind—it will help us discover our life goal and how we might express it to the world. In doing so, we will find the real meaning and significance to our lives.

In fact, it is through us as sentient beings that the universe of latent potential attains conscious manifestation. That is, through us, the universe becomes conscious of itself. As we create greater order and harmony in our lives and grow in awareness, the universe grows bit by bit in order and awareness.

Where is it all going? According to the French Jesuit priest Pierre Teilhard de Chardin, the universe is moving toward what he calls an Omega Point, or a point of optimal order. This is an appealing theory in that, although there is certainly entropy or disorder in the universe (it is scientifically proven to be spreading out), it is also conserving and integrating information into islands of order, as we see in spiral galaxies, complex ecosystems and organisms, and the human brain and mind. We are reminded of what the Sufi mystic Ibn 'Arabi once said: "God sleeps in the rock, dreams in the plant, stirs in the animal, and awakens in man."

And so we are all part of a grand adventure. By doing our part, the universal intelligence flows out from us into the world. In the end, we all make the world a better place. But like the universe, we are a work in progress. We need to give ourselves a break now and then and enjoy the journey. We just keep an eye on our personal goals, and if we find that we've strayed or are fixating too heavily on them, we remind ourselves to slow down and take our time. Then we give full, calm attention to each step before us and to our inner connection.

Blake suffered from depression. He was an intelligent guy who spent most of his time talking himself out of life. When he first entered counseling, he would say things like, "Why bother doing anything, because no matter what you do, it doesn't matter. Life is just a big waste of time." I challenged him on this by noting the fact that he did seek out counseling, so maybe he does care a little. After talking with Blake further, I realized he had an overly utilitarian way of thinking. If he couldn't see the outcome or payoff in something right away, then that something had little or no value. We worked together for several weeks, and Blake became quite proficient at entering calm focus. In quiet moments, Blake would ask his inner mind the important questions such as "What would be a fulfilling thing to do with my life? What could be my life purpose?" Blake complained at first that he was not getting much response. The only thing that would come to mind was an image of him as a child playing in the woods. Blake loved these early times because they allowed him to explore and marvel at nature's ingenuity, particularly the way spiders made intricate webs.

I suggested that Blake meditate on this image further, since it wouldn't keep coming up if it wasn't somehow significant. After doing so, Blake came to the realization of the image. He exclaimed, "I get it now! The spider or the ant doesn't question why it does what it does, it just does it. I need to be like the spider or the ant. If I just stopped overanalyzing and talking myself out of everything, I might find a little contentment." We discussed the possibility of Blake trying this out and seeing what would happen. Blake now designs buildings. Like the spider and the ant, he did what came naturally. He stopped listening to his critical voice (which he later identified as his authoritarian father) and started moving toward what his inner stirrings drew him to.

What this story tells us is that the difference between a random life and a meaningful one depends in large part on how attuned we are to our inner selves. When we are able to "get out of our way" and listen to that still, small voice within, we often find our truth. Our lives then take on meaning far greater than we have previously known. We would all do well to answer the questions "If I imagined my life had deeper meaning and purpose, how would it look? What would I be thinking and doing that I am not doing right now?"

In summary, when we learn to stay in calm focus, we operate in the zone of optimal performance, and many opportunities open up to us that we would not be afforded otherwise. In this calm zone, we have access to a larger awareness that flows into our thoughts and actions, guides us with wisdom, empowers us with choice, and makes things happen. We are able to move with grace above the chaos and transcend our normal limitations.

Glossary

autofocus: A habituated process of perceiving.

awakening: A significant insight or revelation occurring as a result of expanded awareness and contact with a universal intelligence.

broadening focus: Attending to the larger aspects of a situation.

calibration questions: A combination of closed and open questions that ask for confirmation of an inner response.

calm focus: A form of attention that is balanced between relaxation and alertness (relaxed alertness).

central factor: The factor in a problem situation with the most influence; the dominant theme.

closed question: A question that requires only a yes, no, or one-word response.

cognitive overload: A condition of confusion and stress that results from attending to numerous stimuli.

collective unconscious: The term used by the psychiatrist Carl Jung to denote a universal subconscious mind that underlies the connection of all individual minds.

concentrating (narrowing) focus: Attending to the smaller details of one area in a situation.

confirmation bias: A tendency to seek information from a situation that supports a preconceived notion or belief.

contemplative prayer: A receptive form of calm inner focus in which one asks for insight from a larger intelligence.

cosmic consciousness: Expanded awareness arising from making contact with the larger universal intelligence.

current problem state: An emotional or physical reaction to a present difficulty.

decoherence: The process by which quantum waves become progressively entangled with each other and trigger the collapse of multiple-state possibilities into single-state possibilities; the spread of information.

detection markers: Subtle emotional or physical reactions that indicate the presence of a narrow, limited view.

divine guidance: The reception of insight from a larger awareness or intelligence as result of relaxing and broadening focus.

evocation: A triggering of an emotional or physical reaction as a result of immersing in vivid detail.

expanded or nonlocal awareness: Knowledge of things beyond the limits of the physical senses; extrasensory perception.

explicate order: The manifest world of ever-changing form.

false self: A sense of personal identity based solely on the external, sensory-physical world.

fixed focus: A persistent way of perceiving.

flexible focus control: The ability to shift one's viewpoint on command.

framing: Capturing the view of a situation with the least words; getting clear and concise.

habitual reaction points: Common areas where physical tension arises in response to one's current view.

hologram: A three-dimensional image produced by shining a laser through two-dimensional wave patterns; analogy to explain how the three-dimensional universe is produced by two-dimensional quantum wave interactions.

hyper focus: Emotionally charged attention to a single target or stimulus.

immersed mode: A state of mind characterized by absorption in detail.

implicate order: The deeper, hidden dimension of reality that gives rise to the manifest world. (*See* explicate order)

inner dialogue: A creative technique to elicit spontaneous responses from the subconscious or inner mind.

intention: A determined desire for a specific outcome to manifest. (*See also* confirmation bias)

lateral thinking: A nonlinear approach to problem solving; looking at a problem from multiple angles to derive a solution.

life goal: A lifelong pursuit that is an expression of one's true self and which provides deeper meaning and purpose.

mindfulness: A state of mind in which one has transcended conditioned thought and can see clearly things as they are; a state of pure or direct perception; an observant or awakened state. (*See* observer mode *and* situational awareness)

mindfulness meditation: A form of calm inner focus in which one is aware of multiple stimuli at once (i.e., an open focus).

no focus: Wandering attention; the total absence of focus control.

nonlocal space: The outer-dimensional location of the quantum vacuum where matter waves exist beyond this space-time and particles exist in potential.

observer effect: A quantum phenomenon in which one's observation affects the behavior of subatomic particles.

observer mode: A state of mind characterized by a detached perspective; perceiving a situation as a whole.

Omega Point: A term coined by the Jesuit priest Pierre Teilhard de Chardin to refer to the end state of the universe where there will be optimal order.

open focus: Attention to several targets at once. (*See* mindfulness meditation)

open question: A question that requires more than one word, or an elaborated response, to answer.

optimal zone of arousal: An area of mental performance in which there is a balance between relaxation and alertness in which one functions at one's best (a calm focus).

petition or asking prayer: A form of calm inner focus in which one seeks a single outcome from the universal intelligence.

pilot waves: Quantum waves that underlie and influence matter particles.

premature focus: A hasty commitment to a single target (e.g., jumping to a conclusion).

quantum entanglement: The process by which quantum waves interact and share information. Thus, two or more particles may remotely and instantly influence each other (signal-less communication).

quantum information: Information about the state of a particle that is embedded in a particle's waveform; wave patterns or differences in wavelength or frequency.

quantum vacuum: The ground floor of the universe where tiny energy fluctuations wink in and out of existence and produce matter waves.

quantum wave theory: The notion that all matter is comprised of quantum waves of energy and information and that these waves interact to produce everything in the universe.

real problem: The central or major influence in a problem.

resonance: The state that occurs when two or more waves are in the same phase or frequency and there is a sharing of information.

scaling: A numerical rating of one's sense of closeness to a target goal.

scattered focus: Attention to numerous targets or stimuli one at a time (sequential target tracking).

single-point meditation: A form of calm inner focus in which one focuses on the details of a single target, such as a candle flame or the breath.

situational awareness: Knowledge of the larger surrounding environment.

situation overview: An appraisal of the larger aspects and their interrelationship in a problem.

solution state: An emotional or physical state evoked by mentally rehearsing resourceful actions. (*See also* target state)

Solution Targeting: A two-phase problem-solving strategy in which a solution is found by alternating between broad and narrow views of a problem, or between a problem's overall context and its salient details.

superposition: The multiple-state position a subatomic particle can hold within a quantum wave.

sustained or repeated focus: The act of mentally rehearsing resourceful actions over a period of several sessions.

target state: An emotional or physical state evoked by mentally rehearsing resourceful actions. (*See also* solution state)

target actions: The few most effective actions that produce a target (solution) state. (*See also* target markers)

target biases: Familiar thoughts and ideas that are favored and habitually focused on.

target charting: A method of tracking one's current position in relation to a target goal. (*See also* scaling)

target markers: The distinctive thoughts and actions that produce a target state. (*See also* target actions) *target picturing:* Imagining oneself performing in a target state so as to identify its action components.

target resolving or detailing: Examining the individual thoughts and actions involved in a target state.

target sighting: Locating a solution state free of a problem's influence.

target test: The act of determining one's current position in relation to a desired target state through the use of open questions.

thought streaming: The uncensored, free flow of ideas from the inner mind.

true self: One's essential nature that is connected on a deeper level to everything and everyone (the universe-at-large); uniquely integrated quantum information.

unified field: The most fundamental of all nature's fields and the wellspring for both energy and matter; the ground of all being. (*See* quantum vacuum *and* zero-point field)

universal mind: The collective intelligence in the universe arising from or expressed by quantum entanglement and information sharing.

utilization: The act of employing detailed memories of one's own experiences to elicit a resourceful emotional or physical state.

vertical thinking: The act of searching for a solution only from the first view one sees.

visualization: The process of concentrating on and immersing in imagined detail so as to create desired outcomes or intentions.

vortices: Swirling packets of energy that make up subatomic particles.

zero-point field: Lowest level of the universe where quantum energy is produced, even in the coldest vacuums of space. (*See* quantum vacuum *and* unified field)

zooming cycle: One complete shift in focus from a broad view of a problem to a narrow view and back.

zooming in: Mentally concentrating on the details of a subpart of a problem.

zooming out: Mentally stepping back and observing the larger aspects of a problem.

Research
in Distant Mental Effects

Bohm, David. *Wholeness and the Implicate Order*. London: Routledge & Kegan Paul, 1980.

Bohm, David, with B. J. Hiley. *The Undivided Universe: An Ontological Interpretation of Quantum Theory*. London: Routledge, 1993.

Braud, William. *Distant Mental Influence: Its Contributions to Science, Healing, and Human Interactions*. Charlottesville, VA: Hampton Roads, 2003.

Dossey, Larry. *Healing Words: The Power of Prayer and the Practice of Medicine*. San Francisco: Harper San Francisco, 1993.

Lansky, Amy L. *Active Consciousness: Awakening the Power Within*. Portola Valley, CA: R. L. Ranch Press, 2011.

Lommel, Pim Van. *Consciousness Beyond Life: The Science of the Near-death Experience.* New York: HarperOne, 2010.

McTaggart, Lynne. *The Field: The Quest for the Secret Force of the Universe.* New York: HarperCollins, 2002.

———. *The Intention Experiment: Using Your Thoughts to Change Your Life and the World.* New York: Free Press, 2007.

Radin, Dean I. *The Conscious Universe: The Scientific Truth of Psychic Phenomena.* New York: HarperEdge, 1997.

———. *Entangled Minds: Extrasensory Experiences in a Quantum Reality.* New York: Paraview Pocket Books, 2006.

Targ, Russell. *Limitless Mind: A Guide to Remote Viewing and Transformation of Consciousness.* Novato, CA: New World Library, 2004.

Targ, Russell, and Jane Katra. *Miracles of Mind: Exploring Non-local Consciousness and Spiritual Healing.* Novato, CA: New World Library, 1998.

References

Bloch, Douglas. *Listening to Your Inner Voice: Discover the Truth Within You and Let It Guide Your Way.* Center City, MN: Hazelden, 1991.

Bohm, David. *Wholeness and the Implicate Order.* London: Routledge & Kegan Paul, 1980.

Bohm, David, with B. J. Hiley. *The Undivided Universe: An Ontological Interpretation of Quantum Theory.* London: Routledge, 1993.

Bohr, Niels. *Atomic Physics and Human Knowledge.* New York: Wiley, 1958.

Braud, William G. "Distant Mental Influence of Rate of Hemolysis of Human Red Blood Cells." *Journal of American Society for Psychical Research* 84 no. 1 (1990), 1–24.

———. *Distant Mental Influence: Its Contributions to Science, Healing, and Human Interactions.* Charlottesville, VA: Hampton Roads, 2003.

Bucke, Richard. *Cosmic Consciousness: A Study in the Evolution of the Human Mind.* Philadelphia: Innes & Sons, 1905. Distributed by University of Wisconsin Press.

Chopra, Deepak. *How to Know God: The Soul's Journey into the Mystery of Mysteries.* New York: Three Rivers Press, 2000.

Crampton, Martha. "Answers from the Unconscious." *Synthesis Journal* 2 (1975–1978): 140–152.

Dalai Lama. *The Four Noble Truths.* London: Thorsons/HarperCollins, 1998.

Dalloway, Marie. *Visualization: The Master Skill in Mental Training.* Phoenix, AZ: Optimal Performance Institute, 1994.

de Bono, Edward. *Lateral Thinking: Creativity Step by Step.* New York: Harper and Row, 1970.

de Broglie, Louis. *An Introduction to the Study of Wave Mechanics.* London: Methuen & Co., 1930.

de Shazer, Steve. *Keys to Solution in Brief Therapy.* New York: W.W. Norton, 1985.

Dossey, Larry. *Healing Words: The Power of Prayer and the Practice of Medicine.* San Francisco: Harper San Francisco, 1993.

Dyer, Wayne. *The Power of Intention: Learning to Co-Create Your World Your Way.* Carlsbad, CA: Hay House, 2004.

Eddington, Arthur Stanley. *Science and the Unseen World.* New York: MacMillan, 1929.

Erickson, Milton H., Ernest L. Rossi, and Sheila I. Rossi. *Hypnotic Realities: The Induction of Clinical Hypnosis and Forms of Indirect Suggestion.* New York: Irvington, 1976.

Fritz, George, and Les Fehmi. *The Open Focus Handbook: The Self-Regulation of Attention in Biofeedback Training and Everyday Activities.* Princeton, NJ: Biofeedback Computers, Inc., 1982.

Haisch, Bernard. *The God Theory: Universes, Zero-Point Fields, and What's Behind It All.* San Francisco: Wesier, 2006.

———. *The Purpose Guided Universe: Believing in Einstein, Darwin, and God.* Franklin Lakes, NJ: New Page Books, 2010.

Hameroff, Stuart, and Roger Penrose. "Orchestrated Reduction of Quantum Coherence in Brain Microtubules: A Model for Consciousness?" In *Toward a Science of Consciousness: The First Tucson Discussions and Debates,* 507–540. Edited by S.R. Hameroff, A.W. Kaszniak, and A.C. Scott. Cambridge, MA: MIT Press, 1996.

Hiatt, Marta. *Mind Magic: Techniques for Transforming Your Life.* St. Paul, MN: Llewellyn Publications, 2001.

Honos-Webb, Lara. *Listening to Depression: How Understanding Your Pain Can Heal Your Life.* Oakland, CA: New Harbinger, 2006.

Huxley, Aldous. *The Doors of Perception.* New York: Harper, 1954.

———. *The Perennial Philosophy.* New York: Harper and Row, 1945.

International Bible Society. *The Holy Bible, New International Version.* Grand Rapids, MI: Zondervan, 1884.

Jeans, James. *The Mysterious Universe.* New York: AMS Press, 1976.

Jung, C. G. *The Archetypes and the Collective Unconscious.* 2nd ed. Translated by R. F. C. Hull. Princeton, NJ: Princeton University Press, 1980.

Laszlo, Ervin. *Science and the Akashic Field: An Integral Theory of Everything.* 2nd ed. Rochester, VT: Inner Traditions, 2007.

Lommel, Pim Van. *Consciousness Beyond Life: The Science of the Near-death Experience*. New York: HarperOne, 2010.

McFadden, Johnjoe. "The conscious electromagnetic field theory: the Hard problem made easy." *Journal of Consciousness Studies* 9 no. 8 (2002):45–60.

McTaggart, Lynne. *The Field: The Quest for the Secret Force of the Universe*. New York: HarperCollins, 2002.

———. *The Intention Experiment: Using Your Thoughts to Change Your Life and the World*. New York: Free Press, 2007.

Naparstek, Belleruth. *Staying Well with Guided Imagery: How to Harness the Power of Your Imagination for Health and Healing*. New York: Warner Books, 1994.

Patanjali. *How to Know God: The Yoga Aphorisms of Patanjali*. Introduction by Swami Prabhavananda, translated by Christopher Isherwood. New York: Harper, 1953.

Radin, Dean. *The Conscious Universe: The Scientific Truth of Psychic Phenomena*. New York: HarperEdge, 1997.

———. *Entangled Minds: Extrasensory Experiences in a Quantum Reality*. New York: Paraview Pocket Books, 2006.

Robinson, James M., ed. *The Nag Hammandi Library: The Definitive New Translation of the Gnostic Scriptures, Complete in One Volume*. Rev. ed. New York: HarperCollins, 1990.

Rossman, Martin L. *Guided Imagery for Self-Healing*. Novato, CA: New World Library, 2000.

Schrödinger, Erwin. *Mind and Matter*. Cambridge: Cambridge University Press, 1958.

Seife, Charles. *Decoding the Universe: How the New Science of Information Is Explaining Everything in the Cosmos, from Brains to Black Holes*. New York: Viking, 2006.

Shankara's Crest-Jewel of Discrimination. Introduction by Swami Prabhavananda, translated by Christopher Isherwood. Hollywood, CA: Vedanta Press, 1975.

Sharry, John, Brendan Madden, and Melissa Darmody. *Becoming a Solution Detective: Identifying Your Clients' Strengths in Practical Brief Therapy*. New York: Haworth Clinical Practice Press, 2003.

Simonton, O. Carl, Stephanie-Matthews Simonton, and James Creighton. *Getting Well Again*. Los Angeles: J. P. Tarcher, 1978.

Targ, Russell. *Limitless Mind: A Guide to Remote Viewing and Transformation of Consciousness*. Novato, CA: New World Library, 2004.

Targ, Russell, and Jane Katra. *Miracles of Mind: Exploring Non-local Consciousness and Spiritual Healing*. Novato, CA: New World Library, 1998.

Teilhard de Chardin, Pierre. *Christianity and Evolution*. Translated by Rene Hague. New York: Harcourt, Brace, 1971.

Tolle, Eckhart. *The Power of Now: A Guide to Spiritual Enlightenment*. Novato, CA: New World Library, 1999.

Walter, John L., and Jane E. Peller. *Becoming Solution-Focused in Brief Therapy*. New York: Brunner/Mazel, 1992.

William, John K. *The Wisdom of Your Subconscious Mind.* 12th ed.
    Englewood Cliffs, NJ: PrenticeHall, 1973.

Zeilinger, Anton. "Why the Quantum? It from Bit? A Participatory
    Universe?: Three Far-reaching, Visionary Questions from
    John Archibald Wheeler and How They Inspired a Quantum
    Experimentalist." In *Science and Ultimate Reality: Quantum Theory,
    Cosmology, and Complexity*, 201–220. Edited by John D. Barrow,
    Paul C. W. Davies, and Charles L. Harper, Jr. New York: Cambridge
    University Press, 2004.

OVER 125,000 SOLD!

Practical Guide to

CREATIVE
VISUALIZATION

MANIFEST
YOUR
DESIRES

Denning & Phillips

Practical Guide to Creative Visualization
Manifest Your Desires
DENNING & PHILLIPS

All things you want must have their start in your mind. The average person uses very little of the full creative power that is potentially his or hers. It's like the power locked in the atom—it's all there, but you have to learn to release it and apply it constructively.

If you can see it … in your mind's eye … you will have it! It's true: you can have whatever you want, but there are "laws" to mental creation that must be followed. The power of the mind is not limited to, nor limited by, the material world. Creative visualization enables humans to reach beyond, into the invisible world of astral and spiritual forces.

Some people apply this innate power without actually knowing what they are doing, and achieve great success and happiness; most people, however, use this same power, again unknowingly, incorrectly, and experience bad luck, failure, or, at best, an unfulfilled life.

This book changes that. Through an easy series of step-by-step, progressive exercises, your mind is applied to bring desire into realization! Wealth, power, success, happiness, even psychic powers … even what we call magickal power and spiritual attainment … all can be yours. You can easily develop this completely natural power, and correctly apply it, for your immediate and practical benefit.

978-0-87542-183-4, 240 pp., 5³⁄₁₆ x 8   **$12.95**

Meditation

For Beginners

Techniques for Awareness, Mindfulness & Relaxation

STEPHANIE CLEMENT, Ph.D.

Meditation for Beginners
Techniques for Awareness, Mindfulness & Relaxation
Stephanie Clement, PhD

Break the barrier between your conscious and unconscious minds.

Perhaps the greatest boundary we set for ourselves is the one between the conscious and less conscious parts of our own minds. We all need a way to gain deeper understanding of what goes on inside our minds when we are awake, asleep, or just not paying attention. Meditation is one way to pay attention long enough to find out.

Meditation for Beginners explores many different ways to meditate—including kundalini yoga, walking meditation, dream meditation, tarot meditations, and healing meditation—and offers a step-by-step approach to meditation, with exercises that introduce you to the rich possibilities of this age-old spiritual practice. Improve concentration, relax your body quickly and easily, work with your natural healing ability, and enhance performance in sports and other activities. Just a few minutes each day is all that's needed.

978-0-7387-0203-2, 264 pp., 5³⁄₁₆ x 8 $13.95

To order, call 1-877-NEW-WRLD
Prices subject to change without notice
Order at Llewellyn.com 24 hours a day, 7 days a week!

MIND MAGIC

Techniques for Transforming Your Life

" The simple secret of the universe is
you create your own reality."
-Captain Edgar D. Mitchell (Apollo 14 astronaut)

Marta Hiatt, Ph.D.

Mind Magic
Techniques for Transforming Your Life
Marta Hiatt, PhD

Access the incredible, unused power of your mind! Create a life of greater abundance, love, health, and inner peace with life-transforming techniques that really expand your consciousness. There is no power in the world as great as the forces residing in your own mind, and self-hypnosis is a direct pipeline whereby you can release these powers.

A definite, strong idea, when held constantly in the mind, can change the biochemistry of the brain so it will no longer be programmed to failure. Part I of *Mind Magic* explains the nature of consciousness and how the mind works. Part II is a practical handbook on how to apply the theory, with chapters on self-hypnosis, affirmations to attract love and financial success, self-healing techniques, and guided visualizations.

For the skeptic, this book provides a comprehensive understanding of the scientific basis for new-age thought. For the devout, it will provide a thoughtful spiritual base for transformation.

978-1-56718-339-9, 264 pp., 6 x 9   **$15.95**

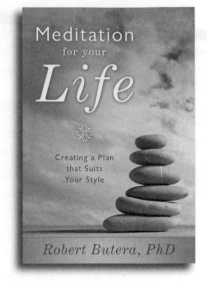

Meditation
for your
Life

Creating a Plan
that Suits
Your Style

Robert Butera, PhD

Meditation for Your Life
Creating a Plan that Suits Your Style
ROBERT BUTERA, PHD

Engage in the process of self-inquiry and understanding with expert teacher Robert Butera. All meditation methods are valid forms of practice, but they don't fit everyone alike. *Meditation for Your Life* explains the six basic forms and guides readers in identifying which ones suit them best. Questions and answers, exercises, and journaling engage readers in learning what steps they can take to make meditation (and its benefits) an enduring part of their lives. Wellness and inner calm are achievable goals with suitable meditation styles—using techniques of breathwork or visualization, mantra or devotion, mindfulness or contemplation. Includes special emphasis on overcoming frequent blocks to inner growth.

978-0-7387-3414-9, 312 pp., 6 x 9   **$16.99**

To Write the Author

If you wish to contact the author or would like more information about this book, please write to the author in care of Llewellyn Worldwide, and we will forward your request. Both the author and the publisher appreciate hearing from you and learning of your enjoyment of this book and how it has helped you. Llewellyn Worldwide cannot guarantee that every letter written to the author can be answered, but all will be forwarded. Please write to:

Keith Park
℅ Llewellyn Worldwide
2143 Wooddale Drive
Woodbury, MN 55125-2989

Please enclose a self-addressed stamped envelope for reply,
or $1.00 to cover costs. If outside the USA, enclose
an international postal reply coupon.

Many of Llewellyn's authors have websites with additional information and resources. For more information, please visit www.llewellyn.com.